ENVIRONMENTAL CRIME

ABOUT THE AUTHOR

Steven C. Drielak received his bachelor's and master's degrees from John Jay College of Criminal Justice, in New York City. As a Senior Investigator with the New York County District Attorney's Office from 1975 to 1978, he investigated cases involving corruption and racketeering. In 1978, he joined the staff of the Suffolk County District Attorney's Office. He was assigned to the newly-created Environmental Crime Unit in May of 1984, and he has command- ed the unit since 1992. During his tenure in the Environmental Crime Unit, he has received two Distinguished Service Awards. Detective Lieutenant Drielak is also a certified instructor for the Criminal Investigations Division of the U.S. Environmental Protection Agency's National Academy and teaches in the Advanced Environmental Crimes Training Program.

ENVIRONMENTAL CRIME

Evidence Gathering and Investigative Techniques

By

STEVEN C. DRIELAK

With a Foreword by

ROBERT F. KENNEDY, JR.

CHARLES C THOMAS • PUBLISHER, LTD.
Springfield • Illinois • U.S.A.

Published and Distributed Throughout the World by

CHARLES C THOMAS • PUBLISHER, LTD.
2600 South First Street
Springfield, Illinois 62794-9265

© *1998 by* CHARLES C THOMAS • PUBLISHER, LTD.
ISBN 0-398-06888-7 (cloth)
ISBN 0-398-06889-5 (paper)

Library of Congress Catalog Card Number: 98-7742

With THOMAS BOOKS *careful attention is given to all details of manufacturing
and design. It is the Publisher's desire to present books that are satisfactory as to their
physical qualities and artistic possibilities and appropriate for their particular use.*
THOMAS BOOKS *will be true to those laws of quality that assure a good name
and good will.*

Printed in the United States of America
CR-R-3

Library of Congress Cataloging in Publication Data
Drielak, Steven C.
    Environmental crime : evidence gathering and investigative
techniques / by Steven C. Drielak ; with a foreword by Robert
F. Kennedy, Jr.
        p.   cm.
    Includes bibliographical references and index.
    ISBN 0-398-06888-7 (cloth). -- ISBN 0-398-06889-5 (paper)
    1. Offenses against the environment--United States. 2. Criminal
investigation--United States. I. Title.
HV6403.D75   1998
363.25'942--dc21   98-7742
                                                                    CIP

To Jo and Kimi

FOREWORD

Not long ago, I sat in my office with Captain Ron Gatto, a New York City Police Officer attached to the City's Department of Environmental Protection (DEP) and charged with protecting the City's upstate reservoir system from pollution. DEP has no authority to prosecute upstate polluters for environmental violations, so when Gatto catches a polluter or developer violating environmental laws, he must persuade a local prosecutor to take the case. A few weeks before our meeting, a worried fly fisherman had alerted Gatto to a noxious plume of milky fluid emitting from a hidden pipe buried in the bank of the Croton River, a feeder tributary to New York's reservoirs. Gatto had traced the pipe to its source, the floor drain in a shop of a Brewster, New York Auto Dealer that regularly ridded itself of dangerous chemicals by discharging them into the drinking water for half the population of New York State. Gatto had taken the evidence first to the local county prosecutor and then to the State Attorney General and the U.S. Attorney. Each, in turn, refused to take the case. Gatto now sat lamenting the lot of environmental crime fighters. "If a kid steals a car or breaks a window with a rock, there's not a prosecutor in the county that won't take the case—and in those cases, there is only a single victim. But if someone dumps poison into the drinking water of 9 1/2 million people, you can't get anyone to prosecute!"

Gatto's complaint is borne out by my own experience and by statistics from across the country. As Chief Prosecuting Attorney for Riverkeeper, Inc., a coalition of commercial and recreational fishermen, I have brought over 100 successful actions against Hudson River polluters, using citizen suit provisions which Congress included in the Clean Water Act and other environmental statutes. Each of these cases was an instance when a corporation or individual or municipality had broken some environmental law. And in each case, the state government enforcement agencies and federal EPA were aware of the violations, some quite serious, and had elected not to prosecute.

Many state governments have virtually stopped prosecuting environmental law violations. In 1996, the state of Maine prosecuted fewer than 50 cases under its environmental laws despite thousands of violations reported to regulators. The state of Virginia prosecuted a single polluter all year and collected less than $4,000 in penalties. Virginia is among the most polluted states in the nation. These states are typical.

The reasons for this failure are manifold. State governments discourage environmental prosecutions in order to recruit polluting industries. Engineers who run environmental agencies often prefer "technical assistance" to prosecution which they deem antagonistic toward problem solving. State and federal prosecutors don't see environmental crimes as "real" crimes like fraud, murder, vandalism, or theft. Most importantly, many prosecutors are intimidated by the difficulties of gathering and preserving evidence and proving environmental crimes with which they are unfamiliar. Steven Drielak's book solves the latter problem. It teaches prosecutors how to collect and preserve evidence, how to prepare a search warrant, perform investigations, and conduct surveillance. It lays out protocols for safety and sampling techniques, methods for interpreting regulatory files and hazardous waste manifests, and how to construct a hazardous waste sting operation.

Environmental crime *is* real crime; improperly disposed pollutants poison community water supplies, contaminate fisheries, and injure human beings. Environmental crime attacks property values, community welfare, and can damage wildlife and human health and rend the social fabric for generations. Since Roman times, western law has held that water and air and wild animals belong to the public. Modern environmental laws simply clarify with particularity the right of the public to safely fish and swim and their entitlement to clean, safe drinking water. When pollution destroys or poisons a resource, the polluter has committed an act of theft against the public. When a contaminated water supply or fishery poisons children—the polluter has committed child abuse. Pollution is crime; polluters must be treated as criminals.

Pollution laws are intended to protect public health, safety, and welfare by ensuring high water quality, enhancing ecosystem health, and reducing pollution by internalizing pollution costs into a discharger's activities. However, merely enacting the regulations will not accomplish any of these objectives alone; only widespread compliance with the law will achieve these goals.

Polluters have no incentive to comply with environmental laws since noncompliance results in economic benefits (the free use of water or air for waste disposal) while compliance exacts a financial cost. Unchecked by aggressive enforcement, these pressures will systematically undermine any system of environmental law. James Elder, the former director of the EPA Office of Water Enforcement and Permits, observed that "[W]e have found repeatedly that nothing is self-sustaining in the National Pollutant Discharge Elimination System (NPDES) program. If a state's vigilance or the EPA's regional vigilance subsides, their noncompliance and point source contribution [of pollution] increase."[1]

Compliance is essential to the success of any environmental regulatory program because it is the only way that society will enjoy the benefits envisioned by environmental laws which legislatures have devised to protect the public. The vast regulatory apparatus we have put in place to protect public health and the environment amounts to mere empty words without compliance. Widespread compliance with environmental law only occurs where society enjoys the deterrent value of strict, sure enforcement. Drielak's book brings this task within reach of every prosecutor.

ROBERT F. KENNEDY, JR.
Supervising Attorney
Pace Environmental Litigation Clinic, Inc.

---

1. James R. Elder et al. *Regulation of Water Quality* 22 Envtl. L. Rep. 10,029-10,037 (Jan. 1992).
2. Cheryl Wasserman, *Federal Enforcement: Theory and Practice Innovation in Environmental Policy,* 21,22 (T.H. Tietenberg ed., 1992).

PREFACE

The art of criminal environmental investigation has seen many changes over the last decade. During its beginning, it would be quite common for a regulatory agency to prepare an environmental criminal case against an individual or corporation and deliver the evidence to a prosecutor. Eventually, trained criminal investigators began working with various regulatory agency personnel in an effort to learn and to better prepare these cases for criminal prosecution. Today, well-trained criminal environmental investigators are taking a proactive approach to environmental crime. New evidence gathering and investigative techniques are continually being developed around the country. These new techniques, combined with the investigator's understanding of the evidence-gathering requirements of the criminal justice system, have begun to produce highly prosecutable environmental crime cases.

This book offers the new criminal environmental investigator numerous investigative techniques which may be applied to a variety of environmental crime investigations. Each of the investigative techniques and evidence-gathering procedures described in this book has been successfully used in criminal environmental prosecutions. I have also attempted to offer information on the numerous safety requirements which *must* be followed in order to safely and properly gather physical evidence at an environmental crime scene. Each chapter has been designed as a reference in order to better assist the criminal environmental investigator with the individual investigative tasks he or she may face in the future.

I would like to thank Special Agent-In-Charge Lori Dueker of the United States Environmental Protection Agency, Criminal Investigation Division, San Francisco Office, for her guidance in the preparation of this book. I would also like to thank Kenneth Hill, Director of the Suffolk County Environmental and Health Laboratory, and Senior Chemist JoAnn Laager for their gracious assistance.

CONTENTS

Page

Foreword by Robert F. Kennedy, Jr.   vii
Preface   xi

Chapter

1. THE CRIMINAL ENVIRONMENTAL   3
    INVESTIGATOR
    Training   3
    Equipment   4
    Standard Operating Procedures   5
    Locating and Utilizing Resources   5
        Safety Resources   5
        Sampling Resources   6

2. SEARCH WARRANTS   7
    Developing Probable Cause   7
        Typical Surveillance   7
        Remote Surveillance   8
        Regulatory Files   14
        Hazardous Waste Manifest System   15
        Regional Enforcement Associations   16
        Worker's Compensation   17
        Unemployment Records   17
        Certificates of Incorporation   17
        Propery Records   18
        Building Plans   18
        Chemical Suppliers Records   18
        Neighboring Businesses   19
        Delivery Services   19
        The Landlord   20
        Multitenant Buildings   20

Page

Planning 21
  Determining Goals 21
  Gathering Evidence 22
  Equipment Requirements 22
  Personnel Requirements 23
The Search-Warrant Team 23
  Crime Scene Coordinator 24
  Site Security Team 25
  Safety Officer 25
  Laboratory Team 27
  Sample Team 28
  Records Team 28
  Interview Team 33
  Raw Chemical Product Inventory Team 34
  Dye Test Team 34
The Briefing 35
  Chain of Command 35
  Safety Officer 35
  Site Investigation Team 36
  Sample Team 37
  Type of Industry 37
  Suspected Hazards 37
  Expected Protection Levels 38
  Decontamination Requirements 39
  Emergency Medical Care 39
  Sampling Operation 40
  Site History 41
  Photographs 41
  Facility Diagram 41
  Weather 41
  Site Security 42
  Communications 43
  Search Warrant Review 43
  Search Warrant Execution 43
  Public Information Officer 44
The Staging 44
  Personnel Check 44
  Operation's Plan Review 44
  Local Police Notification 44

Page

Warrant Execution 45
  Serving the Search Warrant 45
  Establishing Site Security 46
  Parking 46
  Team Deployment 46
  Interior Search 46
  Exterior Search 52
  Postsearch Briefing 54
  Sample Point Identification 55
  Sampling Order 55
  Volume Readings 56
  Chain of Custody 56
  Dye Testing 56
  Releasing Team Personnel 57
  Procecutor 58
  Receipt 58
  Closing the Search Warrant 58
Surreptitious Entry 59
  Disabling Security Systems 59
  Marking Hazardous Waste Containers 60
Postsearch Investigation 61
  Employee Interviews 61
  Chemical Inventory Review 62
  Analytical Evidence Review 62
  Interviewing Suspects 63

3. HAZARDOUS WASTE ABANDONMENT 65
    INVESTIGATIONS
  Notification 67
  Arrival at the Crime Scene 67
  Crime Scene Coordinator 68
  Safety Officer 69
  Safety Team 69
  Decontamination 69
  Emergency Medical Assistance 70
  Sample Team 70
  Laboratory Team 71
  Gathering Evidence in the Hot Zone 71

Page

Postsearch Briefing 77
Chemical Evidence Gathering 77
Abandoned Trailer Investigations 78
Hazardous Waste Tanker Investigations 79

4. DRUM-TRACING TECHNIQUES 83
Vehicle 83
Person or Persons 86
Other Physical Evidence 86
Containers 87
Chemical Analysis 91

5. SAMPLING FOR CRIMINAL EVIDENCE 93
Sampling Plan 93
Sample Bottle Identification and Preparation 94
Sample Device Identification and Preparation 96
Types of Analysis 97
Field Tests 98
Documentation 101
Chemical Evidence Sampling 104
Sampling for Trace Analysis 109
Volume Reading Techniques 112
Photographing Chemical Evidence 116
Labeling Chemical Evidence 116
Sealing Chemical Evidence 117
The Log Book 117
Chain of Custody 118
Chemical Analysis Request Sheet 118
Transporting Chemical Evidence 119
Packaging and Shipping Chemical Evidence 119

6. CHEMICAL ANALYSIS OF CRIMINAL EVIDENCE 121
Choosing the Laboratory 121
Chemical Analysis: Instrumentation and Methodologies 126
Gas Chromatography/Mass Spectrometry 127
Inductively Coupled Plasma/Atomic Emissions 129
Spectrometer
pH Meter 132
Pensky-Martens Close Cup Tester 133

                                                       Page
7. HAZARDOUS WASTE STING OPERATIONS   137
    Targeting Suspect Hazardous Waste Transporters   138
        Planning the Operation   138
        Establishing the Undercover Generator   139
        Hazardous Waste Containers   140
        Hazardous Waste Removal   140
    Targeting Suspect Hazardous Waste Generators   141
        Planning the Operation   142
        Personnel Requirements   142
        The Vehicle   143
        Establishing the Undercover Office   144
        The Criminal Transaction   144
        Examining Hazardous Waste   145
        Disposal   146
        Investigative Files   147

Appendix   149
Glossary   157
Bibliography   165
Table I   167
Table II   220
Index   223

ENVIRONMENTAL CRIME

Chapter 1

THE CRIMINAL ENVIRONMENTAL INVESTIGATOR

TRAINING

A successful criminal environmental investigation requires the application of several different disciplines. The environmental investigator must bring basic police skills such as interviewing and interrogation, surveillance, search warrant execution, and experience in the proper handling of criminal evidence to the investigation. In addition, he or she must be trained and equipped to gather physical evidence at an environmental crime scene, in a safe and proper fashion. This requires specialized training in the handling of hazardous materials and a full understanding of the appropriate environmental laws, supporting regulations, and hazardous waste sampling and analysis protocols.

Fortunately, this specialized training is available to the criminal investigator from a variety of sources. The United States Environmental Protection Agency offers many training programs in the areas of Hazardous Materials Incident Response, Hazardous Materials Sampling, and Criminal Environmental Investigations. Many state and local agencies also offer similar courses. Many of these training programs are free and are offered throughout the country several times a year.

EQUIPMENT

The well-trained, criminal environmental investigator should also be well-equipped. Most successful criminal investigations, be they burglaries, arsons, or homicides, depend upon the investigator's ability to examine and gather physical evidence. Even in situations where evidence technicians are gathering the physical evidence, it is normally done under the direct supervision of the criminal investigator. This same basic investigative principal also applies to criminal environmental investigations. The criminal environmental investigator must be equipped with the proper crime-scene, safety and field monitoring equipment to allow for a safe and proper examination of any physical evidence found at an environmental crime scene. The following is a list of some of the items that may be utilized by the environmental investigator at a crime scene:

- Chemical boots
- Surgical gloves
- Cartridge Respirator
- Fully encapsulating suit
- Chemical suits
- Chemical gloves
- pH Paper
- Duct tape
- Measuring tape
- Steel toed boots
- Overalls
- Dosimeter
- Goggles
- Geiger Counter
- Chemical dictionary
- Binoculars
- First Aid Kit
- Bold markers
- Flashlight
- Bung wrench
- Spark-proof clipboard
- Knife
- Trash bags
- Sterilized sample bottles
- L.E.L./O_2 meter
- Compass
- Communications equipment
- 35mm Auto focus camera
- DOT Emergency Response book
- Self-contained breathing apparatus
- Spare 60 minute air bottle

STANDARD OPERATING PROCEDURES

In addition to obtaining the proper training and equipment, there is a federal requirement to establish *standard operating procedures.*[1] These standard operating procedures must address the issues of health and safety for the environmental investigators working in areas which may contain hazardous substances (see Table I), hazardous materials,[2] and biological hazards.[3]

These procedures should address such topics as organizational work plan, site evaluation, site control, monitoring, personal protective equipment, communications, and decontamination procedures. In addition, it is recommended that standard evidence gathering procedures be incorporated into the standard operating procedures. Such topics as note taking, removal of fingerprints, tire track and footprint castings, the crime scene sketch, crime scene photography, and evidence chain-of-custody procedures should be addressed within the standard operating procedure (see Appendix).

LOCATING AND UTILIZING RESOURCES

One of the most difficult challenges facing the environmental investigator is locating and utilizing the resources necessary to effectively gather evidence at an environmental crime scene. Safety and chemical sampling protocols clearly establish the need for additional personnel with special training.

Safety Resources

Whenever the presence of hazardous substances, hazardous materials, and/or biological hazards is suspected at an environmental crime scene, a qualified safety officer, a backup team, and decontamination facilities are needed. The first step in locating the resources necessary to fulfill these requirements is the identification of the local Hazardous Material Response team (HazMat).[4] The Superfund Amendments and Reauthorization Act of 1986 (SARA), includes an emergency planning provision known as Title III. Under this legislation, each locality in the United States must establish an emergency plan to respond to the release of an extremely hazardous substance. These emergency plans include the requirement for a local hazardous materials response team. In some jurisdictions, the HazMat team may fall under the control of the local fire department, while in others, it may be a function of the local police department. The environmental investigator should locate this team and make every effort to utilize its resources for any environmental crime scene. The environmental investigator may be surprised to find willing and cooperative emergency response personnel. There is a mutual benefit in having HazMat trained criminal investigators and HazMat team emergency responders working and training together. Most HazMat teams are designed to mitigate dangerous situations involving the release or potential release of hazardous chemicals. The HazMat response plan might not have any provisions established to affix culpability on those individuals responsible for the chemical release. When criminal negligence or criminal intent is suspected, the HazMat team should have a qualified environmental investigator available. In addition, environmental crime scenes offer the HazMat team an opportunity to work and train under less than life-threatening situations.

Sampling Resources

The proper gathering of chemical evidence is crucial to the success of any criminal environmental investigation. The personnel utilized for this procedure must be highly trained in safety, hazardous waste sampling and the handling of criminal evidence (see "Sampling for Criminal Evidence" in Chapter 5). Fortunately, many local and state regulatory agencies have such individuals available to assist the environmental investigator. In addition, the United States Environmental Protection Agency has many trained individuals available to assist state and local authorities. The environmental investigator should contact these groups and establish protocols in which their resources may be utilized.

Chapter 2

SEARCH WARRANTS

DEVELOPING PROBABLE CAUSE

When attempting to gather evidence to support an application for a search warrant it is essential that the type of environmental contamination be identified. The facility in question may have air, ground, underground and/or sewer system hazardous discharges taking place. Each type of release has its own unique properties. In gathering probable cause as to their existence, the environmental investigator has a multitude of tools, resources and investigative techniques at his or her disposal.

Typical Surveillance

The typical surveillance involves personnel using vehicles and natural cover in an attempt to personally witness the events taking place at a facility. Still photographs and videotape should assist the environmental investigator in recording these events.

While conducting this type of surveillance, the environmental investigator should note any evidence of past or present discharges which may be seen from his or her surveillance point. Overflowing leaching pools, liquid streams from hazardous waste storage areas, and chemical stains on parking lots may be an indication of illegal hazardous waste release. The exterior walls of the buildings should also be examined for stains. Plating lines, when placed against interior walls, may have their hazardous chemicals leach through those walls. The interior location of plating lines can, at times, be determined by the chemical stains on exterior wall surfaces. Also, the environmental investigator should look for any recent signs of excavation. A long cut in an asphalt or concrete parking lot leading from a building to a storm drain may indicate a recently installed underground discharge pipe. Any sunken or depressed areas around the facility may indicate the presence of a hidden leaching pool. Depressions such as these are normally caused by soil settlement after a leaching pool has been installed.

This type of surveillance will also provide investigators with the vehicle license plate numbers of the various individuals employed at the facility. Once these numbers have been obtained, employee background investigations can begin. These may include criminal record checks and outstanding arrest warrant checks for those employed at the facility. However, there may be times when this type of surveillance is not practical and other methods must be utilized to obtain the desired information.

Remote Surveillance

This type of surveillance comes in many forms. The use of aerial photography, infrared, remote video cameras, or automatic air and sewer samplers allows the investigator to gather a large amount of data while limiting the risk of exposing the investigation.

1. Aerial surveillance of a suspected facility may reveal recent excavation sites, ground stains, manufacturing areas, waste storage, air pollution sources, as well as *point sources* for waste discharges.[5] On occasion, aerial surveillance may also reveal illegal activities in progress (see Figure 1). The use of aerial infrared may be useful in determining underground areas where there is an obvious heat differentiation. It may also assist in locating areas in the facility where certain types of heat-related manufacturing activities are taking place.

Figure 1. An illegal asbestos storage facility. Note the workers' lack of respirators.

2. Remote video cameras have been in use by law enforcement for many years. They are useful in determining if certain types of activities are taking place when ground surveillance is impossible. A telephone pole-mounted video camera, disguised as an electrical transformer, may be useful in determining what activities are taking place at the suspected facility. However, legal restrictions regarding this type of surveillance may differ from state to state. Therefore, it is essential that this type of surveillance operation be reviewed by a prosecutor prior to implementation.

3. Remote air sampling is one of the best methods available today in determining if certain types of chemicals are being used at a facility. Most volatile and semivolatile chemical compounds, when used in quantities or discharged at a facility, can be found in the atmosphere. Today's air sampling devices will allow the investigator to set a timer, leave the area, and return at a later time to retrieve the samples. A chemical analysis of the sample may reveal the presence of these compounds in minute concentrations.

However, using this investigative technique for the gathering of probable cause must be well planned. Many variables may bring into

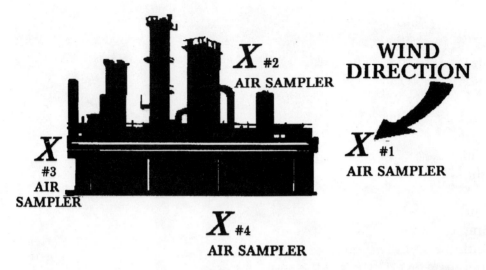

Figure 2. Air sampling devices positioned around a facility suspected of illegally discharging its waste.

question the validity of the sample results. Other nearby manufacturing facilities, vehicle traffic and/or low flying aircraft may contaminate the air sample to such an extent that it is no longer reliable.

The best investigative technique to use in remote air sampling is to place air sampling devices on all four sides of a facility (see Figure 2). Determine and document the wind velocity and direction. Set each remote air sampler to begin air sampling at the same time. This will enable you to determine what air contaminates originated up wind of the facility and which contaminates came directly from the suspected facility.

This technique has been used successfully in cases involving clandestine cocaine manufacturing laboratories. Remote air sampling has been used to show that trace amounts of tetrachloroethylene were coming from a particular building. By surrounding this building with air monitoring devices, it was easy to determine, after analysis, that the building in question was the only possible source of the tetrachloroethylene. The presence of this compound, along with its known use as a precursor in the manufacturing of cocaine, helped supply the necessary probable cause to obtain a search warrant. This same technique can be used to identify chemical usage at various industrial facilities such as plating operations, circuit board manufacturers, furniture strippers, auto body repair shops, and a whole host of other industries utilizing hazardous chemicals that may be indicative of the nature of the business.

4. Hazardous waste discharges to Publicly Owned Treatment Works (POTWs) offer a unique challenge to the environmental investigator. In many cases, the hazardous waste generator will have a permit to discharge certain types of wastes to the POTW.[6] This permit will list the various discharge limitations. In addition, copies of *Discharge-Monitoring Reports* (DMRs), which may be required under the conditions of the permit, may have been filed with the regulatory authority which issued the permit. Copies of these discharge-monitoring reports should be obtained and reviewed by the environmental investigator.

Some generators may exceed the permitted discharge limitations and in some situations, completely bypass any hazardous waste treatment system existing within the facility. This may result in untreated industrial and/or hazardous waste being discharged directly into the publicly owned treatment works. Finding evidence of such releases has become easier in recent years due to improved remote video and sampling technology.

When hazardous waste is discharged into a sewer system, trace evidence may be left behind. The trace evidence may be in the form of scarring and pitting of the discharge pipe's interior. The hazardous waste, especially if it is in the form of hazardous metals, may leave behind a distinct discoloration. Evidence of this may be determined by sending a sled, equipped with a remote video camera, through the system. The video camera may reveal the damage described above. Videotaping of this type of evidence may assist the environmental investigator in gaining the probable cause necessary for obtaining a search warrant.

Portable liquid samplers can be placed into an existing sewer system and retrieved at a later time (see Figure 3). This equipment can be set to automatically sample the waste stream based upon time, flow rates, and/or waste stream characteristics (i.e., pH). The samples are then analyzed and the results of the analysis may be used for probable cause purposes. However, as in the air sampling technique discussed earlier, the investigator must be certain that the suspect facility is the source of the contamination. There may be several businesses discharging into the sewer system. By thoroughly reviewing all available sewer system piping plans, the investigator will be able to determine the proper positioning of the portable liquid sampler. Portable liquid samplers also have the ability to transmit data. If a facility is in the act of discharging hazardous waste with a high (or low) pH, the portable liquid sampler will send a message to a nearby receiving unit. The investigator monitoring this unit will know that the illegal discharge is occurring at that point in time. This is useful in situations when law enforcement personnel wish to catch the suspect facility in the act of discharging.

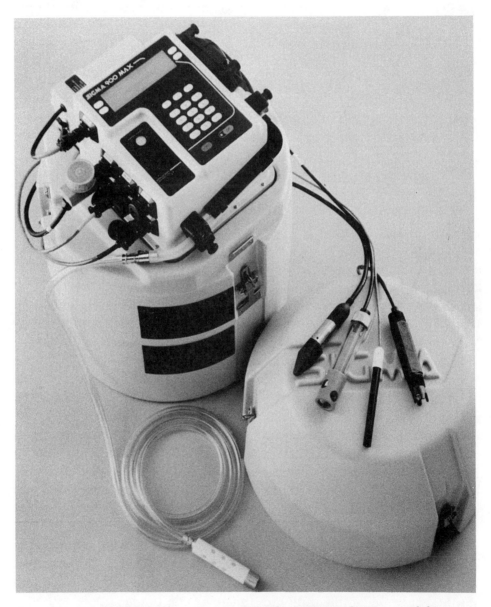

Figure 3. Portable liquid waste sampler with remote notification capability.
Photograph courtesy of American Sigma.

If the above technology is not available to the environmental investigator, there is an additional technique available. A sample team may covertly enter the sewer system and physically retrieve a sample. As with the use of the portable liquid sampler, the environmental investigator must be sure that the point being sampled can be directly traced to the suspect facility.

This type of surreptitious sampling operation is usually done at night and through some entry point in the street. This type of operation will take a great deal of planning due to the risks involved with sampling hazardous waste within a confined space. There are numerous state and federal confined space regulations that govern this type of activity (see Figure 4).[7] In this type of surreptitious operation, the safety of the entry personnel must be of primary concern. In addition, any violations of existing confined space regulations and/or laws on the part of the environmental investigator will diminish his or her credibility at trial. It is important to remember that law enforcement personnel *may not violate the law to enforce the law.*

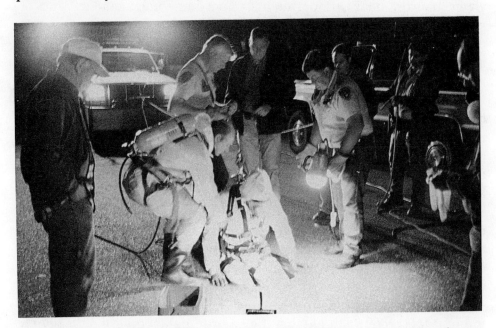

Figure 4. An improper confined-space entry into a POTW sewer line. An air line-supplied respirator with winch and tripod are required here.

Regulatory Files

Regulatory files are a very good source of information that may assist the investigator in establishing probable cause. On a local level, vast amounts of information concerning a specific facility may be found in fire inspection records, fire department records, building inspection records, health department inspection records, local water board records, and state environmental agency files.

1. Local fire inspection records may indicate an inventory of hazardous chemicals present at the facility. Building inspection records may reveal the presence of hazardous vapor venting systems. In cases involving air pollution, this type of information may be vital to the environmental investigator.

2. The best source of information regarding a facility's environmental history may be found in regulatory air permit files, waste water discharge permit files, and related hazardous waste management files. Inspections for these programs may have been completed by local water boards, health departments, environmental agencies, and/or public works departments. In some jurisdictions, it may be the state environmental regulatory agency that completes the majority of these inspections. In other instances, you may find that a federal inspection was completed by employees of the United States Environmental Protection Agency (US-EPA). In each instance, the inspector should be located and interviewed regarding what he or she may have seen at the facility during the inspection process. The inspection files may contain information as to type of industry, chemical raw product inventory, hazardous waste inventory, air release limits, water release limits, facility management, as well as information regarding how any hazardous waste produced by the facility is disposed of. This may include the name of the licensed hazardous waste transporter utilized by the facility. The environmental investigator may then contact the hazardous waste transporter to determine if the suspect facility has been properly shipping out its hazardous waste. Discretion should be exercised, as this may alert the suspect facility as to law enforcement's interest. It is recommended that the environmental investigator review hazardous waste shipment information by utilizing the data in the Hazardous Waste Manifest System.[8]

3. When attempting to build probable cause for a search warrant, there is one regulatory agency that must not be overlooked. That

agency is the Occupational Safety and Health Administration (OSHA). This agency receives thousands of complaints each year from employees concerned about workplace safety. Many of these complaints involve the use and/or misuse of hazardous chemicals in the workplace. The information contained in these files may lead the environmental investigator to employees and former employees who are willing to be interviewed regarding possible illegal activities occurring at the facility under investigation.

4. Another source of information which should not be overlooked is the local Emergency Planning and Community Right-To-Know Act[9] database. This federal legislation was enacted in 1986. One of its purposes is to help increase the public's knowledge of and access to information on the presence of hazardous chemicals in their communities. This Act requires certain facilities with quantities (>500 pounds) of *Extremely Hazardous Substances*[10] and large quantities (> 10,000 pounds) of *Hazardous Substances*,[11] to submit a list of these chemicals or the Material Safety Data Sheets for these chemicals, to the Local Emergency Planning Committee, State Emergency Response Commission, and the local fire department. In some jurisdictions, this database may be maintained by the local Hazardous Material Response team or the local emergency preparedness office. This database may assist the environmental investigator in determining what specific chemicals (and quantities) are present at a specific facility.

Hazardous Waste Manifest System

This system was designed to track hazardous waste from cradle to grave. It requires certain generators of hazardous waste to fill out a multipart *Hazardous Waste Manifest*. This document provides information on the amount and type of waste being removed from the facility. It also lists the hazardous waste transporter's name. The generator must keep a copy of the manifest and give the remaining copies to the transporter. Once the hazardous waste has reached its final disposal site, a copy of the manifest is sent to the regulatory agency. It is at this point that the manifests, in many states, are placed into an accessible computerized database. However, it should be noted that some state databases may be lacking in up-to-date information regarding recent hazardous waste shipments.

Copies of a facility's hazardous waste manifests may be found in several locations. A copy of the manifest is normally kept by the generator (facility), the transporter, the treatment facility, and the state of origination. By examining the originating state's manifest database, the environmental investigator can determine the following:

1. Dates of hazardous waste removal.
2. Amounts of hazardous waste removed.
3. The types of hazardous waste removed.
4. The method of removal (i.e., drums or tankers).
5. The transporter utilized for removal.
6. The treatment, storage, and disposal facility which received the waste.

This allows the environmental investigator to research the hazardous waste disposal history for a particular facility. There may be a dramatic decrease in the volume of hazardous waste shipped from the facility in a year-by-year comparison. There may be no record of hazardous waste ever being shipped from the facility. This type of information is vital to the environmental investigator. If he or she can establish that raw hazardous chemical products are being utilized at the facility and there is no record of hazardous waste being shipped out, there may be probable cause to believe that the hazardous waste is being stored or disposed of illegally.

There are very few industries that can utilize hazardous chemicals, yet create no hazardous waste. However, it is possible that an on-site waste treatment and/or reclamation system exists. Information regarding these systems may be found in the regulatory files. However, it is incumbent upon the investigator to obtain additional probable cause beyond that which is offered by the hazardous waste manifest system.

Regional Enforcement Associations

There are four regional environmental enforcement associations within the United States. These associations are:

• Midwest Environmental Enforcement Association
• Northeast Environmental Enforcement Project
• Southern Environmental Enforcement Network
• Western States Project

These associations have joined together to create an environmental database. This database is known as the Regional Associations

Information Network (RAIN). The information contained in this database includes the *Criminal Pointer System*. This system consists of information regarding state and local criminal environmental actions filed throughout the United States and member Canadian Provinces. Environmental investigators may search via modem for information regarding a suspect company or individual. Database access information may be obtained by contacting one's local regional enforcement association.

Worker's Compensation

This database supplies information regarding employees work-related injuries. In some jurisdictions, the database may be accessed by the name of the employer. However, one may need the name of an individual employee to obtain the information desired. This database can supply the environmental investigator with the names of current and former employees at a particular facility who have been injured on the job. In some cases, the injury may be due to chemical exposure. These records, combined with interviews of any injured employees, may provide additional information needed to establish probable cause.

Unemployment Records

The value of interviewing former employees cannot be overstated. These individuals have the potential for supplying detailed information as to the day-to-day operations at a suspect facility. Information regarding the manufacturing process, hazardous chemical inventory, and waste disposal may be obtained through interviews with these individuals.

Certificates of Incorporation

Certificates of Incorporation normally indicate the type of business that is being conducted by the corporation. These certificates will also provide information regarding the legal name of the corporation. This legal name is vital when it is time to prepare the search warrant and the search warrant application. These records are normally filed with the Secretary of State, for each individual state. In addition, numerous commercial services exist that can supply detailed corporate information regarding individual companies. This information can include the number of persons employed, corporate credit history, and detailed information regarding management personnel.

Property Records

Property records are essential in determining the exact location of the suspect facility. These records will assist the environmental investigator in describing the property's location for the search warrant and the search warrant application. These records may also indicate when the property was purchased. Knowledge of the prior owners and operators of a particular suspect facility may be essential as the investigation progresses. It is a common practice today to blame any environmental contamination found at a facility on the prior owners and/or operators.

Building Plans

In many locations throughout the United States, it is a local requirement that builders of commercial buildings file engineering plans with the local city, town, or county government. These plans often contain engineer's drawings showing the exact locations of air stacks, freshwater plumbing, waste-discharge pipes, sanitary pools, and connections to sewers and storm drains. The environmental investigator should make every effort to have any existing engineering plans available during the execution of the search warrant.

Chemical Suppliers Records

It may be difficult to determine the exact types of hazardous chemicals being used at a facility. Simply knowing that the facility in question is using a *press wash* may not be sufficient for probable cause purposes. Press wash normally contains hazardous chemical solvents. However, the exact type of solvents and their percentage present in the product, may vary by chemical supplier. Therefore, it is vital that the chemical supplier utilized by the suspect facility be identified. This may be accomplished in three ways:

1. A telephone survey of all local chemical suppliers may be productive. A listing of chemical suppliers may be found in the *OPD Chemical Buyers Directory.*[12]

2. Surveillance of the facility may detect a drum storage area. Through the use of binoculars, the environmental investigator may be able to note the name of the chemical supplier as listed on the labels of the drums.

3. A thorough examination of the facility's trash may produce the name of the chemical supplier. However, evidence obtained under these circumstances may come under future legal review. The environmental investigator must make every effort to strictly follow the laws that govern this type of law enforcement activity. It may become necessary to take the local trash removal company into your confidence. If the suspect facility's trash is picked up and placed into an empty truck and then later examined by the environmental investigator, it is unlikely that any successful legal challenge could be made.

This same technique may be used when it is suspected that the facility is mixing their hazardous waste and trash together. However, it is essential that the prosecutor review any plan regarding this type of evidence-gathering procedure.

Neighboring Businesses

Interviews of the surrounding businesses may be of value to the environmental investigator. These individuals may have witnessed suspicious activities such as discharges to storm drains, installation of outside waste pipes and/or the presence of chemical odors at specific times of the day or night.

Delivery Services

Surveillance of the facility may reveal numerous deliveries being made. These deliveries may include office supplies, spare parts and/or refills for any vending machines. The delivery personnel have had the opportunity to make observations while inside the facility and may be a valuable source of information for the environmental investigator.

The Landlord

Many commercial businesses rent the space that they are occupying. The landlord, having a vested interest in the property, may be cooperative in supplying information to the environmental investigator. In many cases, it is the landlord who has brought forth the initial complaint regarding environmental problems at a suspect facility. It is also common for the landlord to be the complainant in a situation where the tenant has abandoned the facility and left behind quantities of hazardous waste. In cases such as these, the investigator should proceed with caution: if there is a bankruptcy involved, it is possible that the former business has listed its hazardous waste with the bankruptcy court and the criminal intent on the part of the former tenant may be questionable. However, if a bid for hazardous waste removal was received by the generator prior to the bankruptcy proceeding and the hazardous waste was abandoned at the site, it still may be possible to pursue criminal charges against the generator. Cases involving any bankruptcy issues should be thoroughly reviewed by the prosecutor.

It is also important to determine if the tenant has had access to the building after his or her business ceased operations. If the landlord has changed the locks on the building, the former tenant may not have been afforded an opportunity to remove the hazardous waste. This may prevent the establishment of criminal intent. Cases such as these may be best left to the civil courts and the regulatory agencies.

Multi-Tenant Buildings

Multi-tenant buildings add significant challenges to the environmental investigator who is attempting to enter a specific suite or area in the building. These problems are usually compounded by the fact that many of the tenants may share the same waste discharge system. It may be necessary to obtain a search warrant for each tenant in the building. If a hazardous waste discharge to a joint leaching pool is suspected, it will be necessary to execute a search warrant at each tenant's facility. Using evidence gathered during the searches, the suspect tenant will, in all likelihood, be isolated and identified based upon chemical sample analysis.

PLANNING

The execution of an environmental search warrant requires an extraordinary amount of planning on the part of the environmental investigator. Due to the nature of the evidence being gathered (hazardous waste), it is essential that every effort be made to safeguard the health and safety of all members of the search-warrant team as well as employees at the facility. There are many steps to be taken in the planning stage. Each step is designed to meet the many problems and obstacles that may arise during the execution of an environmental search warrant.

Determining Goals

Criminal environmental investigations cover a wide range of statutes. These statutes may be on a local, state, or federal level and may involve the illegal transportation, treatment, storage, and/or disposal of hazardous waste. Illegal activity may include ground water contamination, air pollution, ground discharges, discharges to publicly-owned treatment works, illegal landfills, and/or water pollution. The contaminates involved may be hazardous wastes, acutely hazardous wastes, hazardous substances, extremely hazardous substances, hazardous materials, construction and demolition debris, medical waste, industrial waste, and/or household trash. Once the type of waste, as defined by the statute, has been identified, the environmental investigator must research and understand what type(s) of samples and analysis will be needed to meet the requirements of that particular environmental statute. These sample types may include specific metals, specific organic chemicals, acids, caustics, flammable liquids, petroleum, phenols, and polychlorinated biphenols. Each sample type may require special sampling protocols and sample containers.[13] The analysis requirement may include the use of *gas chromatography/mass spectrometry, inductively coupled Plasma/atomic emissions spectrometry, pH* readings and *Ignitability* tests. In addition, these statutes may require that specific weights and volumes of the wastes be present.

When the environmental investigator is armed with this knowledge, he or she will then be able to gather the proper evidence needed to obtain a criminal conviction.

Gathering Intelligence

The safe and successful execution of an environmental search warrant may depend on information that may not be evidentiary in nature. When possible, it should be determined if any individuals at the facility are licensed to carry firearms. Having this information prior to the execution of a search warrant may avert a misunderstanding and possible tragedy. If it is the intent of the environmental investigator to execute the search warrant while the manufacturing process is in operation, he or she must be absolutely clear as to what time the facility opens and begins its operations. If it is the environmental investigator's intent to execute the warrant during nonoperating hours, he or she must be aware of any security systems that may exist. This includes armed guards, alarm systems, video surveillance cameras, and guard dogs.

Equipment Requirements

Due to the unique nature of the evidence being gathered (hazardous) and the locations where it is usually found (pipes, drums, tanks, tankers, leaching pools, underground tanks), it is essential that the environmental investigator determine his or her equipment needs carefully. Exposing and sampling a 3,000 gallon leaching pool containing hazardous waste will require particular types of equipment. However, sampling a 5 million gallon leaking petroleum tank, 75 feet above the ground, with winds gusting to 30 mph, will require an entirely different set of equipment. In addition to the sampling equipment required (see "Sampling for Criminal Evidence" in Chapter 5), the following is a listing of just a few of the items that may be needed during the execution of the search warrant:
- Level "A" safety equipment
- Level "B" safety equipment
- Level "C" safety equipment
- Confined space safety equipment
- Decontamination line
- Emergency medical equipment
- Back hoe
- Picks and shovels
- Ladders

- Lights
- Generator
- Compressed air supply
- Metal detector
- Ground penetrating radar
- Remote drum opener
- Non sparking hand tools
- Jackhammers
- Video camera
- Vegetable dye
- Communication system
- 35mm camera
- Compass
- Measuring tape
- Duct tape
- L.E.L. meter
- O_2 meter
- Geiger counter

Personnel Requirements

Personnel planning is one of the most important elements in preparing for the execution of an environmental search warrant. Each member of the search-warrant team has a specific role to play in the execution of an environmental search warrant. Having too many individuals at an environmental search warrant scene may be more damaging than not having enough. Having untrained and unqualified personnel at an environmental search warrant may be dangerous to all involved. A simple rule should apply in these situations: *If you do not have a specific job to do, you don't go!*

THE SEARCH-WARRANT TEAM

The successful execution of *any* criminal search warrant depends on those assigned to the operation. The environmental search warrant is no different. Each team member must be properly trained and certified within their discipline. Severe damage to the prosecution's case may result if it is later determined that the personnel at the scene were not properly trained in the handling of hazardous materials or that the sample teams were not properly trained and certified in the taking of hazardous waste samples.

In addition to having qualified personnel present, a clear chain-of-command must exist. However, this command structure must have a built-in flexibility to change at a moment's notice.[14] Due to the hazardous nature of the evidence being gathered, the simplest evidence gathering operation may turn disastrous at any moment. With this command flexibility, each team member is aware of *who's in charge* at any given moment during an emergency (see Figure 5).

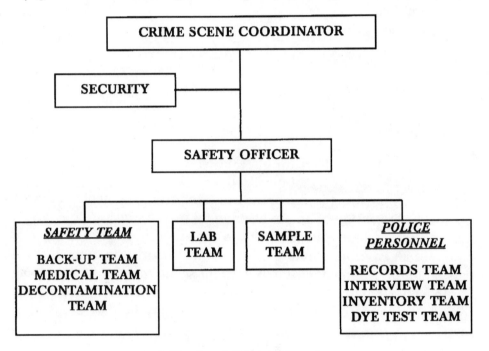

Figure 5. The Search-Warrant Team Structure.

Crime-Scene Coordinator

The position of crime-scene coordinator is held by the primary criminal environmental investigator assigned to the investigation. This person is charged with the ultimate responsibility for the success or failure of the investigation. This responsibility must come with decision-making authority. The actual duties and responsibilities of this individual will vary from case to case. However, certain basic duties can be applied to all environmental search warrants. Some of these include:

- Conducting a briefing prior to the execution of the search warrant.
- Making all team assignments.
- Controlling the paperwork at the scene.
- Conducting all conversations with any legal representatives appearing on behalf of the facility.
- Conducting a *postsearch briefing* prior to the sampling operation.
- Giving final approval for the *sampling plan* prior to the commencement of any sampling operation.
- Inspecting all evidence prior to its removal from the facility.
- Conducting a safety, equipment and personnel check prior to the closing of the search warrant scene.
- Issuing a receipt for evidence removed, if required.

Site Security Team

The *uniformed* site security team has two major functions. First, they will enforce whatever facility employee entry/exit policy that has been established prior to the execution of the search warrant. If, for example, it has been predetermined that employees may leave at any time, but not return, it will be the responsibility of the site security team to clearly and firmly communicate this policy to those affected.

The second major function of the site security team is to enforce, if necessary, any *obstruction law* which may be violated by individuals at the facility. If an employee or member of management conducts themselves in such a way as to interfere with the execution of the search warrant, it may become necessary for the site security team to remove such a person from the site. The site security team should report to, and be in continuous communications with, the crime-scene coordinator.

Safety Officer

Having a safety officer at a suspected hazardous waste site is mandated by OSHA regulation.[15] All issues regarding safety are the responsibility of the safety officer during the execution of an environmental search warrant. This individual must be thoroughly trained in the handling of hazardous materials. If the execution of the search warrant requires hazardous waste sampling in confined spaces, then this individual must also be trained in the area of confined space entry. The site safety officer should control the HazMat backup team, the medical team and the decontamination team. This person will also determine what level(s) of personal protective equipment will be worn and any decontamination procedures to be followed during the execution of the environmental search warrant. *No hazardous waste sampling operation should commence without the safety officer's knowledge and approval.* It is essential that the safety officer and crime-scene coordinator be in continuous communication with each other throughout the execution of the search warrant.

Safety Team

This team, under direct supervision of the site safety officer, may be comprised of the following personnel:

HazMat Backup Team

The HazMat Backup Team acts as support and emergency rescue for those individuals working within a designated *hot zone, confined space* or both.[16] If the sample team consists of two individuals working within one of the above described areas, there must be at least two individuals acting as their Backup team.

Decontamination Team

The environmental investigator may find extremely hazardous chemicals at certain environmental search warrant sites. These chemicals may include *acutely hazardous wastes* (see Table I). Due to the toxicity of these compounds, it may be necessary for all personnel exiting the hot zone to follow a predetermined decontamination procedure. These procedures may include a simple removal and bagging of contaminated clothing or it may be necessary for all personnel exiting the hot zone to go through a multiple wash-down procedure.

Medical Team

Deciding whether or not to have a hazardous material-trained Medical Team at an environmental search warrant site will depend on many factors. The site's physical layout, the location of the nearest medical facility, the volatility, reactivity and/or toxicity of the waste involved, levels of protection and weather conditions should all be taken into consideration. If a Medical Team is present, they should fall under the direct supervision of the safety officer.

Laboratory Team

This team should consist of one or two qualified forensic chemists. Their responsibilities begin long before they actually enter an environmental search-warrant site. Each and every piece of equipment that is to be used for the gathering of chemical evidence must be thoroughly inspected and sterilized prior to leaving its storage facility. A full record of this procedure should be maintained. Once at the search-warrant site, this same laboratory team will keep records as to what samples have been taken, what scientific field tests have been conducted and the results of these tests. A log of the sampling methodology utilized by the sample team should be kept. In addition, they will make every effort to maintain the integrity of the chemical evidence by following procedures which would rule out any possibility of cross-contamination or outside contamination.

If a team such as this is utilized, they should take custody of the chemical evidence at the closure of the crime scene and transport it to a laboratory or evidence storage area. These individuals must be properly trained in the handling of hazardous materials and criminal evidence.

Science Officer

It is recommended that a qualified individual be appointed site science officer during any chemical evidence gathering operations. By utilizing the most senior forensic chemist in this fashion, the environmental investigator will be adding to the technical resources at his or her disposal during the execution of the search warrant. The site science officer, the site safety officer, and the crime-scene coordinator must work jointly throughout the warrant execution in an effort to insure that all of the chemical evidence is gathered safely and properly.

Sample Team

Sample team operations are by far the most difficult and dangerous activities conducted during an environmental search warrant execution. The proper sampling for chemical evidence goes far beyond simply putting liquids or solids into sample containers. Each step of the chemical evidence gathering operation is highly regulated.[17] Any deviation from the countless recommended procedures may result in a devastating cross-examination by a defense attorney at trial. Sample team members must be cognizant of their personal safety, the possibility of chemical evidence cross-contamination, the proper sampling methods, and the issues surrounding the proper chain-of-custody for any chemical evidence seized. It is essential that this team receive frequent rest periods throughout the duration of the environmental search warrant.

Each member of the sample team must be trained in the handling of hazardous materials, confined space certified, and should also have received formalized training in the proper methods of taking chemical evidence samples. In addition, each member of the sample team should be trained in the handling of criminal evidence.

Records Team

The records maintained at a suspect facility may prove vital to the success of an environmental investigation. In many instances, these records will provide evidence of *knowledge* and/or *motive* on the part of the suspect. Any search made for these records should be conducted by trained criminal investigators. Records indicating the installation of illegal waste discharge pipes or air pollution discharge systems will greatly enhance the prosecution's case. In addition, locating a written estimate for proper hazardous waste removal may help the environmental investigator to establish a financial motive for the crime.

When seizing these records certain basic evidence gathering techniques should be followed. Prior to the removal of any documentary evidence, the evidence should be photographed. In addition, a sketch should be drawn which indicates the areas to be searched. This sketch should include any offices, desks and/or file cabinets that are to be searched. A numbering and/or *grid system* should be used so that each seized document can be readily associated with the area from which it was seized. A complete inventory should be maintained during the seizure process and continually reviewed by the records team supervisor to insure that the records seized are in compliance with the limitations set forth in the search warrant. If the records team supervisor finds a document already seized and inventoried that does not meet the criteria set forth in the search warrant, he or she should cross it off the inventory list and return it to its original location. The records team supervisor should then initial the crossed-out entry on the inventory list. This procedure will help insure that the investigators do not seize records that are not authorized by the search-warrant. Also, if the search warrant execution procedures should be reviewed by a court at some future time, this procedure will be indicative of the records team's *good faith* efforts in following the parameters set forth in the search warrant.

The records team should make every effort to locate and seize the following documentation:

Material Safety Data Sheets (MSDS)

The Material Safety Data Sheets offer a wide range of information to the criminal environmental investigator. When these records are seized during the execution of an environmental search warrant, the investigator may be able to determine what hazardous chemicals are being used in the manufacturing process. The Material Safety Data Sheets will also list other names by which the chemicals may be known (i.e., 2 propanone = acetone). In addition, information may be listed on the Material Safety Data Sheets indicating a particular chemical's characteristics. If the MSDS indicates a flashpoint of 75°F, the environmental investigator may wish to request that an Ignitability Test be conducted on the seized chemical evidence.[18] If the MSDS indicates that the chemical has a pH of 1.5, the environmental investigator may wish to request that an Electronic pH Test[19] be conducted on the seized chemical evidence.

The MSDS may also provide a key element needed for the prosecution's case. Each MSDS lists the individual hazards for that particular chemical. It may also indicate what procedures are to be followed to lawfully dispose of any hazardous waste by-product. If these documents were to be found in the suspect's office, it may be an indicator that the individual had *knowledge* as to the chemical's properties and proper disposal procedures. If the documents were found in the suspect's desk, it would further strengthen the prosecution's case.

The *Federal Hazard Communications Standard* requires that employers have a Material Safety Data Sheet for each hazardous chemical they use and that copies be maintained in the workplace.[20] The MSDSs are to be readily accessible during all shifts and they are to be maintained in the employee work areas. This may provide the environmental investigator with a starting point in his or her attempt to locate and seize these documents. However, it is also common to find these records in office areas. The environmental investigator may find them attached to shipping papers, purchase orders, and/or purchase requisitions.

Raw Chemical Product Purchases

One of the key ways to estimate how much hazardous waste is actually generated at a facility is to examine the raw chemical product purchases. A large increase in the purchase and usage of raw chemical products may indicate an increase in hazardous waste production.

It is common for facilities with illegal hazardous waste discharges to claim that the hazardous waste found during the search warrant is due to some form of outside contamination. The suspect may claim that the individual chemical compounds found in the chemical evidence samples have never been utilized in the manufacturing process. These raw product purchase records, along with the Material Safety Data Sheet information, may assist in countering any such claims made by the suspect.

Hazardous Waste Manifests

It is a federal requirement that the generators of hazardous waste maintain a copy of their hazardous waste manifests for three years.[21]

By searching for and seizing these records, the environmental investigator may be able to establish several key points concerning the investigation:

• If no manifests are found at the facility, it may be an indication that there has been no legal shipment of hazardous waste in the last three years or,

• There has been legal shipment of hazardous waste from the facility; however, no copies of the manifests have been maintained by the generator or,

• Any completed manifests found at the facility will help establish *knowledge* on the part of the generator as to the proper hazardous waste disposal procedures.

Regulatory Reports and Correspondence

On many occasions, the environmental investigator may find that the suspect facility has had numerous dealings with a local, state, or federal environmental regulatory agency. These files may contain prior inspection reports, laboratory reports, notice of violations and/or correspondence. These records may indicate that the suspect was aware that hazardous waste was being generated at the facility and that the hazardous waste was required to be disposed of properly.

Environmental Surveys

The most common motive in environmental crimes is one based upon financial gain. It is common for a generator of hazardous waste to hire an outside consulting firm to thoroughly review the facility's hazardous waste management and then reject the consultant's recommendations based upon financial reasons. These written recommendations may indicate proposed on-site treatment systems, piping and plumbing schematics, estimates of waste generation, disposal methods, and the projected costs associated with each of these items. It is also common to find laboratory analysis of the waste stream in these reports and files. Each one of these items may be helpful in supporting a future prosecution position that individuals at the facility had both *knowledge* and *motive* when committing the environmental crime.

However, when attempting to seize documents of this nature, the environmental investigator must be aware of all *Self-Audit Privilege* laws that may exist within that jurisdiction. As of 1996, many states had passed laws making environmental self-audit reports privileged information. In some jurisdictions, this privileged status has made these reports inaccessible, absent a waiver or court order, to law enforcement agencies.[22] The environmental investigator and prosecutor should thoroughly examine this issue prior to the execution of the search warrant.

Accident Records

These records are useful in determining which, if any, employees have been injured at the facility. Some of these employees may no longer be employed by the facility and may be willing to discuss the operation of the facility with the environmental investigator at some future time. Those injuries involving hazardous materials and/or hazardous waste should be examined thoroughly by the environmental investigator.

Personnel Records

These records may contain the names, addresses, job descriptions, job titles, and employment history of both past and present employees. These records may also contain information regarding environmental and/or hazardous materials training that individuals within the facility may have received. Proof of this type of training may assist the environmental investigator in establishing knowledge on the part of various employees and management personnel. Utilizing these records will help reduce the investigative time needed during the post search warrant investigative phase. These records may assist the investigator in determining which employees are directly involved with the manufacturing process as well as those employees functioning in a supervisory capacity.

Equipment Logs

Information contained in equipment maintenance logs may be crucial to the investigation. This is especially true when there is an on-site hazardous waste treatment system. Any records indicating the nonfunctioning of such a waste treatment system may later become vital when attempting to show the causation of any hazardous waste discharge.

Interview Team

It is a standard police procedure to identify those individuals present at a search warrant scene. However, simple identification may be insufficient. By utilizing a roving interview team during the environmental search warrant execution, each employee can be approached and interviewed. A custom-designed employee interview sheet that allows the interviewing investigator to collect needed information can be of great value in this situation. If the interviewee is willing, an instant photograph should be taken of the employee and attached to the interview sheet. This will assist the investigator in employee identification during any future interview process. The interview sheet should contain questions covering the following topics:
- Name
- Address
- Date of birth
- Home telephone number
- Length of employment
- Past vacation dates
- Work schedule
- Job description
- Immediate supervisor
- Management names and duties
- Equipment used by employee
- Chemicals used in the manufacturing process
- Hazardous waste disposal procedures
- Work-related injuries
- Procedures followed for accidental chemical releases
- Procedures followed when government inspectors arrive

Utilization of the interview team concept may provide the environmental investigator with the following benefits:
- Once the employee has made statements as to the facility's operation, it will be difficult for that individual to change his or her statement at a later time.

• The interview process will identify key supervisory and management personnel in the manufacturing and hazardous waste handling areas.

• The number of postsearch-warrant, follow-up interviews will be reduced based upon what is learned by the interview team.

• Interviewed employees may express an interest in speaking with the investigator at a later time and/or in a more private setting.

Raw Chemical Product Inventory Team

The hazardous chemical inventory is one of the most important functions of the entire evidence gathering operation. If, for example, the environmental search-warrant team finds 1, 1, 1 Trichloroethane waste in a leaching pool, it is essential that they also find the raw chemical product utilized within the facility. The records of purchase of raw 1, 1, 1 Trichloroethane are corroborative in nature. However, a sample and analysis of the raw chemical product is the best evidence that the investigator can deliver to the prosecutor.

Dye Test Team

There are many ways to prove that certain piping and plumbing discharge to a particular location. However, the easiest and most efficient way to prove this is to introduce a vegetable dye into the suspected piping system and await its arrival at the suspected end point. This should be done by two individuals who are in constant communication with each other. The event should be recorded with the date, time, dye color, investigators' names, and a full description of the entry and discharge points. Under no circumstances should the dye be introduced prior to the sampling operation. This will avoid having to prove at a later date that the dye was benign in nature. Crime scene photographs and/or a videotape showing the colored dye entering the suspected discharge point may be of great evidentiary value to the prosecution.

SEARCH WARRANTS: THE BRIEFING

The search warrant briefing is a critical part of the warrant execution process. Many individuals from different agencies may be brought together in an effort to collect evidence in a safe, efficient, and legally admissible manner. It is essential that each person on the team be made aware of what his/her role is and by what manner the assigned tasks are to be accomplished. It is at this juncture that input is received from all members of the search-warrant team and based upon this, the final operations plan is developed.

Federal law requires that a written emergency response plan be developed and implemented to handle anticipated emergencies prior to beginning any hazardous waste operations.[23] The search-warrant briefing may be utilized to satisfy this requirement. It is recommended that the briefing be held by the crime-scene coordinator at least 24 hours prior the to execution of the warrant. This will allow ample time in the event that changes must be made based upon any new incoming information. At a minimum, the following topics should be addressed during the search warrant briefing:

Chain-of-Command

The crime-scene coordinator and his or her executive officer are identified. Each team member will be made aware that the crime-scene coordinator will have absolute authority over the search-warrant execution. If the crime-scene coordinator should become incapacitated during the environmental search warrant execution, the Executive Officer will assume command.

Safety Officer

The site safety officer shall be selected and identified at the briefing. The role of the safety officer is to be fully explained to all present at the briefing. It must be made clear that this individual shall assume full command of the search warrant scene in the event of an emergency. In addition, it must be made clear to all members of the search-warrant team that any area containing possible hazardous waste contamination is not to be entered with out the knowledge and approval of the safety officer.

Site Investigation Team

This group of individuals will search the facility's interior and exterior for environmental violations. Each site investigation team is to be made up of four individuals. Each of these individuals will have been trained in a different discipline. The site investigation team should consist of:

Environmental Investigator

This individual is well-versed in the applicable environmental statute(s) and will determine what evidence must be gathered to corroborate the case. In addition, this individual will bring his or her expertise in the area of detecting illegal hazardous waste discharges. This individual will make the determination as to whether or not a particular area or item will be sampled for evidence of hazardous waste. The environmental investigator will also decide the types of analyses that are to be conducted as they relate to each sample point.

Sample Team Member

The sample team member will evaluate each sample point in an effort to ascertain his or her sampling equipment needs. It is important to note that a hazardous waste tank, a 55-gallon drum and a sink elbow will all require different types of sampling equipment in order to obtain the needed chemical evidence.

Forensic Chemist

The forensic chemist will act as scientific advisor throughout the search process. In addition, this individual will consult with the environmental investigator as to the different types of chemical evidence analyses needed for each individual sample point.

Safety Team Member

The function of this individual is to evaluate each sample point for any possible safety hazards. The sampling of tanker trucks, underground pits, leaching pools, and 55-gallon drums all represent different hazards that may face the sampling team. This individual will address such safety concerns as levels of protection, fire and explosion hazards and confined space entry requirements for each individual sample point.

Sample Team

The sample team(s) will be established at the briefing. It is here that the lead sampler(s) will be named. These individuals, along with an assistant sampler(s), will conduct all chemical evidence gathering activities during the execution of the search warrant.[24] The lead sampler for each sample team should be the individual who has the most experience in gathering chemical evidence for *criminal prosecution purposes*. In all likelihood, this individual will be called to testify at trial regarding the protocols and methods used to gather the chemical evidence.

Type of Industry

The search-warrant team should be thoroughly briefed as to the type of business being conducted at the suspect facility. Plating operations, furniture refinishers, auto body shops, printing operations, circuit board manufacturers and dry cleaning operations all utilize different processes. They also utilize different chemicals during those processes. Therefore, having some basic knowledge as to how the suspect facility's system operates will greatly assist the entire search-warrant team in locating and seizing chemical evidence.

Suspected Hazards

Based upon the information developed during the probable-cause phase of the investigation and having a basic knowledge as to the type of industry about to be searched, a listing of suspected hazardous chemicals can be created. Once this list has been created, the proper Material Safety Data Sheets may be obtained for each individual chemical substance. This is especially important when one or more of the suspected hazardous chemicals falls under the category of acutely hazardous waste. Each member of the search-warrant team should be supplied with copies of the relevant MSDSs.

Expected Protection Levels

Personal Protection Equipment (PPE) levels will be established based upon the type of industry and MSDS information. It is always a good policy to plan for the unexpected by bringing equipment of at least one level of greater protection than is indicated by the MSDS. Therefore, if the suspected hazardous chemicals at the site require Level "C" protection equipment, then Level "B" safety equipment should be brought to the site. Likewise, if the suspected hazardous chemicals at the site require Level "B" protection equipment, then Level "A" safety equipment should be brought to the site.

If the purpose of the search warrant is to gather chemical evidence regarding the illegal discharge of an acutely hazardous waste, then a Level "A" protection should be considered. This type of evidence-gathering operation is both difficult and dangerous. The inherent properties of Level "A" protection equipment (total encapsulation) makes evidence gathering a difficult task (see Figure 6). Limited sight, limited mobility, high interior suit temperatures and allowable working time all impact the individual's ability to gather evidence. In addition, the very nature of the evidence being gathered (acutely hazardous waste) makes this operation a dangerous one. *If at all possible, Level "A" evidence gathering operations should be avoided.* However, if it should become necessary to utilize this level of protection in order to gather the chemical evidence, it is essential that the operation be conducted by well trained and experienced personnel.

Figure 6. Level "A" operation involving acutely hazardous waste.

Decontamination Requirements

Decontamination needs will be established at the briefing. The types of hazardous wastes involved, as well as any MSDS information, will help to determine the decontamination requirements. These may range from a simple stripping and bagging of contaminated clothing, to a full decontamination line equipped with scrubbing areas, rinsing areas, and waste water containment.

Emergency Medical Care

Each search-warrant team member will be advised as to the location of the first-aid station. The first-aid station should be utilized for minor injuries only. The location of the nearest medical facility should also be established during the briefing. In the event of a Level "A" evidence gathering operation involving acutely hazardous wastes, it is recommended that an ambulance, staffed by qualified emergency medical technicians, be present during the execution of the search warrant.

The Sampling Operation

Each suspected sample point should be evaluated during the search warrant briefing. It is during this evaluation that the various types of chemical evidence to be seized will be established. In addition, the required sampling equipment necessary to gather the chemical evidence will be discussed.

Various analytical tests may be required depending upon the types of chemical evidence being seized. Some of these analytical tests may include:

- Volatile Organic Compounds
- Semi-Volatile Organic Compounds
- Total metals
- Corrosivity
- Ignitability
- Total Characteristic Leaching Procedure (TCLP)
- Total Petroleum Hydrocarbons (TPH)
- Polychlorinated Biphenols (PCBs)

Each of these analytical tests may require special chemical evidence gathering techniques and chemical evidence containers. In many instances, the number of samples planned for is exceeded by the number of samples actually taken during the course of the environmental search warrant execution. This is due to the fact that the extent of hazardous waste discharges cannot be established in advance. Therefore, it is essential that extra chemical evidence gathering equipment and containers be brought to the site.

The issue of *split samples* may be addressed during the search warrant briefing. This involves the collection and handing over of *physical evidence* to a suspect at an environmental crime scene. While this type of conduct is extremely rare during standard criminal investigations (i.e., homicide, narcotics, arson, sex crimes), the taking of an extra set of samples for the suspect may be required under local law and in some limited federal regulatory situations.[25] The criminal environmental investigator must be cognizant of what the *law requires* regarding split samples and differentiate this from any regulatory policy. He or she must recognize that the taking of nonessential chemical evidence samples will increase the sample team's exposure time to the hazardous waste and/or acutely hazardous waste being sampled. Factors such as physical stress, weather, in-suit temperatures, chemical suit and glove permeation rates, and general fatigue must all be evaluated prior to the making of this type of decision. If it is determined, after discussions with the prosecutor, that no such legal requirement for the taking of split samples exists, then *no split samples should be taken!*

Site History

A complete review of the site's history should be made at the briefing. It is common to have numerous types of industries occupying the same physical location over a period of months or years. Knowing what types of industry formerly occupied the site may help the search-warrant team differentiate between old chemical discharges and any newer ones committed by the current facility operator.

Photographs

All ground and aerial surveillance photographs should be reviewed by each member of the search-warrant team. These photographs will assist in the pinpointing of sample points and in determining where to locate the first-aid station and the equipment-setup and decontamination areas.

Facility Diagram

A diagram of the facility, based upon surveillance and intelligence information, should be drawn and reproduced for each member of the team. The diagram should indicate all buildings on the site and all suspected discharge points, hazardous chemical storage areas, hazardous waste storage areas, manufacturing areas, and administrative offices. The diagram should include a map legend indicating points of direction.

Weather

Proper weather conditions are a critical component for the successful execution of an environmental search warrant. Projected outside temperatures as well as wind direction and velocity should be determined in advance. The weather forecast for the warrant execution date should be distributed to each member of the search-warrant team.

Adjustments in the search warrant execution date and/or time should be considered if the weather conditions are expected to have a negative impact on the health and safety of the search-warrant team members or on the collection of evidence. Very cold temperatures may freeze hazardous waste, making it difficult to obtain a proper sample. These same cold temperatures may affect electronic sensing equipment such as L.E.L./O_2 meters and freeze water lines in the decontamination system. Snow covered ground may hide discharge pipes and leaching pools that would normally be visible. Heavy rainfall may be channeled into the same area as the illegal hazardous waste discharge, making proper sampling difficult. Extreme heat may have a devastating effect upon sampling team and backup team personnel. On hot days, individuals wearing chemical suits may be facing extremely hot in-suit temperatures, possibly leading to medical problems for these individuals and jeopardizing the entire operation.

Some of these problems may be overcome with careful planning. If extremely cold conditions exist, a heated command post can be established in a bus or truck to protect personnel and equipment from the elements. An air-conditioned command post may be established under hot conditions. Sample team and backup team members can be equipped with a simple flagman's vest with disposable chemical ice packs in the interior pockets. The vest may be worn under a chemical suit and will assist in maintaining a cooler in-suit temperature.

Site Security

The decision to close (or not to close) a facility during the execution of a search warrant is a difficult one. Regardless of what the ultimate decision is, it shall be enforced by the site security team. Each member of the search-warrant team should be made aware of this decision at the briefing.

In deciding to close (or not to close) a facility, many factors must be evaluated. The issues of search-warrant team safety, facility employee safety, and the potential for the destruction of evidence all must be evaluated. The environmental investigator must also be mindful of the fact that the search warrant is an evidence gathering tool and *not* an accusatory instrument. Closing a facility, even for a short time, may have a major impact on the future operation of the company.

One of the best methods for handling this situation is to have the operating facility closed to anyone wishing to enter but, at the same time, allowing anyone inside the facility an opportunity to leave whenever they wish. However, those who do leave will not be allowed to re-enter until all evidence gathering has been completed. This policy may effectively *reduce* the number of individuals inside the facility for the duration of the search warrant. In addition, the criminal environmental investigator must make every effort to avoid any situation which allows for an *increase* in the number of individuals within the facility during the duration of the search warrant as this may result in numerous distractions and unforeseen problems.

Communications

As with any major law enforcement operation, good communications are essential. The crime-scene coordinator, safety officer, science officer, investigation teams, records team, interview team, and security team must have the ability to communicate effectively with each other. The best way to accomplish this is with a hand-held radio system set to a dedicated channel. This information should be distributed to the entire search-warrant team at the briefing.

Search Warrant Review

While the briefing allows for the final search warrant operations plan to be formalized, it is important to make certain that the plan meets all of the criteria set forth in the search warrant. The search warrant's itemized list of areas to be searched and evidence to be seized should be compared with each team's assignment. This is especially important to the records team and sample team. Each member of the search-warrant team must be made aware of *where* they are allowed to search and *what* evidence they are allowed to seize as dictated by the parameters listed in the search warrant.

Search Warrant Execution

The facility's location, search warrant execution date, execution time and staging area location should be provided to all search-warrant team members at the briefing.

Public Information Officer

If a public information officer is to be made available during the environmental search warrant execution, then that individual should be present at the search warrant briefing. This will provide the public information officer with a basic understanding of the search warrant execution plan.

THE STAGING

On the day of the environmental search warrant execution, all those who are assigned to the search-warrant team should meet at a predesignated time and place. The staging area should be located close to the facility that is about to be searched. By utilizing a staging area, the environmental investigator will be able to accomplish several important last-minute tasks.

Personnel Check

This provides the environmental investigator with an opportunity to insure that all required personnel are present. If an individual member of the search-warrant team is not present, this will afford an opportunity to have that individual replaced prior to the execution of the search warrant.

Operation's Plan Review

It is possible that new information may have been received during the time period between the search warrant briefing and the staging event. The operation's plan review provides an opportunity to address the entire search-warrant team as to any newly arrived data and/or change in plans.

Local Police Notification

It is essential that the local police be notified just prior to the execution of the search warrant. This is especially true when the search warrant is in, or borders on, a residential area. Marked environmental and hazardous material response team units may cause alarm on the part of the neighboring community. It is quite common for the local police to be inundated with telephone calls regarding the search warrant activities at a facility. This notification will provide the local police with the necessary information they need to answer any inquiries made by concerned citizens. In addition, the name and telephone number of the crime-scene coordinator should be supplied to the local police. This will enable the communication of any new information from the local police to the crime-scene coordinator. This is especially helpful should an individual contact the local police with new information regarding the facility.

THE WARRANT EXECUTION

An orderly progression of events is essential when executing an environmental search warrant. Without this orderly progression, the environmental investigator will find the search-warrant team personnel and their equipment scattered about the facility in an unorganized state. By following the search warrant execution plan as set forth in the briefing, each individual will know exactly what duties to perform upon their immediate arrival.

Serving the Search Warrant

When executing an environmental search warrant at an operating facility, the crime-scene coordinator and uniformed members of the site security team should inform a representative of the facility as to the search warrant's existence. A copy of the search warrant may be shown to the representative. A copy of the search warrant should be given to a facility representative if such a requirement exists under local law. It is at this point that the facility representative will be informed of the policy decision regarding the continued operation of the facility during the environmental search warrant execution.

If the crime-scene coordinator believes that there is a possibility for a confrontation or violence during the initial serving of the search warrant, he or she should have the remaining search-warrant team members stand by at the staging area. Should the crime-scene coordinator and the site security team encounter hostility, the safety of the other team members can be assured.

Establishing Site Security

Once notice of the search warrant has been served, the site security team should take up security posts at the facility's entrances and exits. If there is a concern for the possible destruction of documentary evidence, then a security post should be immediately set up in the area in question. If there is a concern for the possible tampering of evidence in the manufacturing area, then a security post should be established there as well.

Parking

Once the facility has been secured, the crime-scene coordinator should summon the remaining search-warrant team members waiting at the staging area. Upon their arrival, the safety officer will determine the exact positioning of vehicles and equipment. These decisions may be based upon wind direction, availability of a fresh water supply and suspected sample points. Every effort should be made to avoid having the search-warrant team members inadvertently parking their vehicles over contaminated storm drains, leaching pools, and/or piping.

Team Deployment

Once the positioning of vehicles and equipment is completed, the individual teams may be deployed. The records team, interview team, raw chemical product inventory team and the site investigation team should begin their operations.

Interior Search

The four-person site investigation team should begin their search on the inside of the facility. They should proceed in such a way as to insure a compete search of the entire interior including the attic and basement areas. As the team moves through the facility, they should be evaluating each identified sample point for:

- Evidentiary value (environmental investigator).
- Types of analysis needed (forensic chemist).
- Sampling equipment needed (sample team member).
- Safety equipment needed (safety team member).

Waste Discharge Points

Waste discharge points may be found in the form of sinks, toilets, floor drains, holes in the walls, holes in the floor and/or air venting systems (see Figures 7 & 8). The environmental investigator may find that many of the discharge points have been hidden under or behind heavy equipment. The floor should be checked for scratches and marks which may indicate that the heavy equipment has been moved often. Holes in the floor and walls should be examined for temporary plugs or patches.

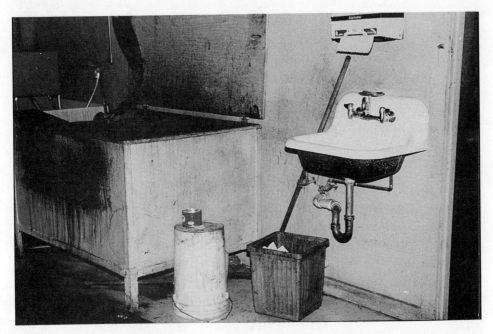

Figure 7. A typical slop sink used as a hazardous waste disposal point.

Figure 8. A hidden hole in the floor is used as a hazardous waste disposal point.

All sinks and toilets should be examined for chemical stains and scarring. This is an indication that some form of chemical waste may have been discharged through this point. If a suspected sink is found, the sink's elbow should be identified for sampling.

All piping from suspected discharge points should be traced to its ultimate outflow point. This piping system should also be checked for valves that would allow the waste to be diverted to another location. If the suspected waste pipe runs above ground level (i.e., attached to the walls or ceiling), any low-point should be identified for sampling. These low-points may accumulate small amounts of hazardous waste. A sample may be obtained by drilling a small hole into the pipe.

Any suspected pumps and hoses should be identified for seizure (see Figure 9). Their exact location in the facility should be noted on the crime scene sketch. If it is suspected that the pump and hose has been used to drain a hazardous waste tank or drum(s), exact measurements should be taken between these items and the suspected discharge point (i.e., sink or stormdrain). The hose should then be measured to insure that it has the necessary length which would enable it to transfer the hazardous waste from a tank(s) or drum(s) to the suspected discharge point.

Any technical information listed on the pump should be noted. This includes the name of the manufacturer and model number of the pump. The *gallons per minute* (gpm) rating should also be noted. If an employee should state that the pump was run for two hours per day, the environmental investigator will then have evidence as to how much hazardous waste was actually discharged (pump rating of 1 gpm x 60 min = 60 gals. Per hr., 60 gals. x 2 hrs. =120 gals. per day).

Figure 9. Seized pump used to transfer hazardous waste from a storage tank to a storm drain.

All waste storage areas should be examined by the investigation team. It is quite common for facilities to combine their hazardous waste with some other waste such as waste oil and trash. If a waste-oil storage area is located, it should be identified and sampled.

Any *drum rings* on the floor should be noted and marked for photographs. This is an indication that drums had, at some point, been stored in this location. This information may become valuable during the follow up interviews with employees.

The site investigation team should locate and identify for sampling any raw hazardous chemical product that may have been used in the manufacturing process. They should coordinate their efforts with the raw chemical product inventory team. If the raw hazardous chemical product is packaged in small volume containers, the entire container should be seized as evidence and analyzed.

Any on-site hazardous waste treatment equipment should be thoroughly examined (see Figures 10 & 11). All internal, incoming and outgoing piping from this type of equipment, should be examined and traced. The site investigation team should examine this equipment for signs of use and for any plumbing which would allow the system to be bypassed.

Figure 10. A nonfunctioning hazardous waste treatment system. Note the case number and investigator's initials written in the dust.

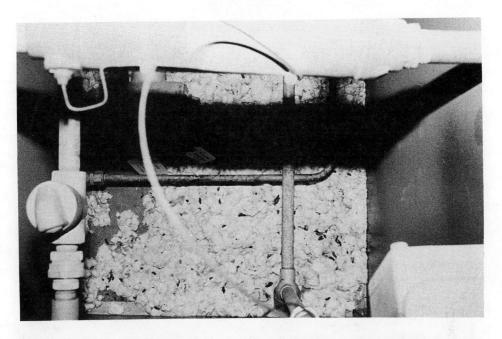

Figure 11. Note the interior rat's nest and rat droppings inside this hazardous waste treatment system.

In addition to on-site treatment facilities, many hazardous waste generators may have their own laboratory capabilities. These on-site laboratories are normally used to analyze the generator's waste stream. In situations where a federal or state discharge permit is required, the analysis information may be used for discharge-monitoring report (DMR) purposes. The filing of DMRs with a regulatory authority may be required under the terms of the permit.

The equipment in the laboratory should be examined and inventoried by qualified search-warrant team personnel. The entire laboratory and all equipment should then be photographed. The laboratory's analytical capabilities should be noted and compared to any analytical reports issued by the laboratory. If, for example, the on-site laboratory had issued DMRs indicating that lead, cadmium and chromium were *not* present in the waste stream, the environmental investigator will want to insure that the laboratory had the capability of performing these types of analysis. The lack of the proper analytical equipment may call into question the validity of the discharge-monitoring reports.

Exterior Search

Once the site investigation team has completed their search of the interior of the building, they should proceed to the surrounding outside area. This search should also be conducted in a systematic way. Each leaching pool and storm drain should be found and examined (see Figure 12). All visible pipes exiting the building, including roof drains, should be traced, if possible, to their outflow point.

Figure 12. A site-investigation team located this storm drain receiving an active flow of hazardous waste.

When examining a suspected leaching pool or storm drain, the environmental investigator should determine if the pool is one that is capable of leaching its contents into the ground. It may be difficult to tell, without close examination, if the pool in question is not, in fact, a storage tank. The walls should be visually examined and the bottom probed to determine if it is capable of leaching its contents. The interior should also be examined for any pipes entering or exiting the system. By examining these pipes, the environmental investigator may be able to determine the direction from which the pipes originate. A measuring device should be used to determine the *exact* diameter of the pool (see "Sampling for Criminal Evidence: Volume Reading Techniques" in Chapter 5). A record of this measurement, including the name of the individual doing the measurement, should be maintained. This information will be vital in determining the amount of liquid hazardous waste in the pool.

All ground areas should be examined for asphalt patches, concrete patches, depressions, and recent excavation. A depression in the ground may indicate soil settlement over a pool cover. If the pool cover is equipped with a metal lift ring, its exact location my be determined by use of a metal detector. In addition, a long steel rod may be used as a soil probe to help determine the pool cover location.

All ground stains should be examined as possible sample points. When dealing with a large contaminated area, the dimensions of the area should be recorded. In addition, the depth of contamination should be determined and recorded. This may be accomplished by taking samples at different depths in the soil. This procedure should be repeated at several points within the contaminated area. The stain dimensions, combined with the depth of contamination and the weight of the sample will determine the poundage or tonnage of contaminated soil present. This may be vital if the local criminal environmental statutes have a requirement regarding amounts of hazardous waste present.

All raw hazardous chemical product storage areas, both inside and outside the facility, should be examined and identified for possible sampling (see Figure 13). All hazardous waste storage areas should be examined for leakage and identified for possible sampling. In addition, all trash receptacles and other solid waste containers should be examined for hazardous waste contamination. The roof of the facility should be examined for piping systems, hazardous waste storage and air pollution sources.

Figure 13. Raw-product storage areas such as this one must be
inventoried and sampled.

Postsearch Briefing

The postsearch briefing is required under federal regulations.[26] This
briefing should be attended by the crime-scene coordinator, safety
officer, science officer, all safety team members, and sample team
members. In addition, members of the records team, chemical raw
product inventory team, and interview team should be in attendance.
It is at this point that each team makes a report to the crime-scene
coordinator and the safety officer.

It is during this postsearch briefing that each sample point will be
decided upon. The types of analyses needed for each sample point will
also be determined. Sampling and safety protocols will be set for each
drum, pool, pipe, sink elbow, floor drain, point source, and soil sample. Each sample point must be approved by the site safety officer and
the crime-scene coordinator. It is recommended that the safety officer
and the crime-scene coordinator personally view each sample point
prior to the commencement of the sampling operation.

Sample Point Identification

Each sample point should be clearly identified with a field sample point number placed on a sampling placard (see Figure 14). The first digit on the placard refers to the number for that particular sample point. The next two letters are the initials of the lead sampler. The last numbers are the date. The placards should be placed at each sample point prior to sampling. This will assist the sample team in clearly identifying the sample point at which they are collecting chemical evidence. In addition, each sample point and placard should be photographed. The location of the sample points and the field sample point number should be noted on the crime-scene sketch. The field sample point number will be the control number utilized for chemical evidence identification and chain-of-custody purposes.

Figure 14. Typical sample point placard used to identify individual sample points.

The Sampling Order

When deciding the sampling order, the crime-scene coordinator and the safety officer should attempt to have the most difficult samples taken first. Certain sample points may require Level "A" protective equipment. Other samples points may require a confined-space entry. Weather conditions and available lighting conditions may also play a role in determining the sampling order. It would be unwise to have a tired sample team, in Level "A" protective equipment, removing acutely hazardous waste samples under poor lighting conditions. It is these types of considerations that must be addressed when determining the appropriate sampling order.

Volume Readings

It is essential that accurate volume readings be taken at each sample point. When sampling leaching pools, storm drains and other discharge points, an accurate measurement of the amount of hazardous waste present is vital. It is recommended that at the completion of a particular sampling point, the sample team make a measurement of the liquid present. Taking measurements such as this after the chemical evidence has been removed may avoid any future claim of cross contamination which may have been caused by the measuring technique. The amount of liquid present, the field sample point number and the name of the individual making the measurement must be recorded (see "Sampling for Criminal Evidence: Volume Reading Techniques" in Chapter 5).

Chain-of-Custody

During the course of the environmental search warrant execution, the sample team may take dozens of chemical evidence samples. The sampling process may take many hours to complete. These facts, combined with a meal period and frequent rest periods may add to the potential for a break in the chain-of-custody. It is vital that the chain-of-custody be maintained throughout the execution of the search warrant.

Dye Testing

Dye testing should commence at the *conclusion* of the sampling operation (see figure 15). Each suspected sink, toilet, floor drain and suspected hazardous waste discharge point should be tested in this manner. It is recommended that a different color of vegetable dye be used for each suspected discharge point. All dye testing points should be noted on the crime-scene sketch.

Figure 15. A vegetable dye was introduced into a hidden interior floor drain and was then photographed flowing into this exterior leaching pool.

Releasing Team Personnel

Certain members of the search-warrant team may finish their assignments prior to the completion of the sampling operation. Members of the records team, interview team, and raw product inventory team should be released from the site at the completion of their duties. However, prior to leaving the site, these individuals must meet with the crime-scene coordinator and make a report as to any evidence seized and/or information obtained. Before any search-warrant team member leaves the facility, the safety officer should be notified and the individual's name and time should be recorded.

Prosecutor

It is recommended that the prosecutor visit the site prior to the completion of the search-warrant execution. This will afford the him or her an opportunity to obtain a better understanding of the case he or she is about to prosecute. Crime-scene photographs and videotapes, although informative, do not offer the same perspective as a personal viewing. The prosecutor should receive a full briefing from the crime-scene coordinator. The prosecutor should arrive at the facility *after all evidence gathering activities have ceased.* This avoids the possibility of the prosecutor becoming a witness in his or her own case.

Receipt

Some jurisdictions may require that a general receipt be left at the facility for any items seized during the execution a search warrant. If such a requirement exists, the amount of samples removed, pumps, hoses, records, and any other items seized during the execution of the warrant should be recorded on the receipt. It is recommended that carbon paper be used when filling out the receipt. This will provide the crime-scene coordinator with an exact copy of the receipt left at the facility. When possible, the receipt should be given to a member of the facility's management. That individual's name should also appear on the receipt.

Closing the Search Warrant Scene

Once the receipt has been issued to the facility's representative, the crime-scene coordinator and the safety officer should inspect the interior and exterior of the facility. They should remove any contaminated material and/or equipment inadvertently left behind by members of the search-warrant team. The interior and exterior should also be inspected for any hazards left behind by the search-warrant team. An uncovered storm drain or leaching pool may cause serious injury or even death to an employee or visitor at the facility (see Figure 16).

Figure 16. This sewer entry port was inadvertently left open after the sampling operation. It was discovered just prior to the closing of the crime scene.

SURREPTITIOUS ENTRY

Law enforcement has been utilizing surreptitious-entry warrants for many years. The primary use for this type of search warrant has been to install audio and/or video surveillance equipment within a specific location. However, within recent years, the increased investigation of environmental crimes has introduced new situations for which such a warrant may be useful.

Disabling Security Systems

The environmental investigator may find it necessary to disable the security system at a facility prior to the execution of a search warrant. Many manufacturing facilities have outside video surveillance cameras. This will allow the employees of the facility to view the search-warrant team prior to their entry into the building. This will also afford the employees of the facility ample time to cease any active discharge of hazardous waste that may be in progress. In order to maintain the element of surprise, it may be necessary to obtain a surreptitious-entry search warrant in addition to the environmental search warrant. This will enable law enforcement personnel to enter the facility surreptitiously and disable the surveillance system prior to the execution of the environmental search warrant. This type of operation is normally executed in early morning hours prior to the opening of the facility. The surveillance equipment must be disabled in such a way as to prevent it from being repaired immediately. The execution of a surreptitious entry warrant, in conjunction with an environmental search warrant, requires careful planning and precise execution.

Marking Hazardous Waste Containers

The environmental investigator may learn that hazardous waste containers, such as 55-gallon drums, located at a specific facility, are about to be disposed of illegally. It may be advantageous to the investigation that some form of identifying mark be placed on these containers prior to their removal. If, at some future point, these containers are abandoned and/or in the possession of some unauthorized person, the point of generation can be clearly determined by examining the identifying mark.

If it is suspected that such disposal is imminent, and if the existing evidence can support this type of operation, a surreptitious-entry warrant should be obtained. In this situation, the facility should be entered under the cover of darkness and when the possibility of discovery is at its lowest point. Marks should be placed on the containers in such a way as to be unnoticeable by anyone handling the containers at a later time. One way to accomplish this is to contact the local crime laboratory in advance. A specialist in the identification of tool marks should be consulted. The specialist can prepare a set of bolt cutters by serrating the cutting edge. An example of this unique cutting edge mark should then be placed onto a piece of test metal. This piece of metal, with its unique tool mark, should then be saved as evidence.

The surreptitious-entry team can use this set of bolt cutters to place their unique mark on the lip edge of any hazardous waste containers at the site. However, a great deal of caution should be exercised when attempting this type of operation. Personal protective equipment and the proper air monitoring devices must be utilized at all times. Also, a properly equipped backup team should be standing by in the event of an emergency.

Should the hazardous waste containers be abandoned and/or come into the possession of some unauthorized person, the unique mark found on the containers can be compared to the unique mark made on the piece of test metal in the crime laboratory. These identical tool marks will clearly establish that the hazardous waste containers are the same containers marked by the environmental investigator during the execution of the surreptitious-entry warrant.

The environmental investigator may be tempted to obtain samples of the hazardous waste through the use of a surreptitious entry warrant. This can be a very complicated operation and is not recommended. Safety requirements, sampling equipment requirements and decontamination requirements make this type of sampling operation extremely difficult to accomplish under surreptitious conditions.

POSTSEARCH INVESTIGATION

The execution of the environmental search warrant may provide the criminal investigator with the evidence foundation needed to proceed with the investigation. All seized records, employee statements, analytical evidence, and personal observations made during the environmental search warrant execution must be thoroughly examined. Once this seized evidence has been reviewed, the criminal investigator should attempt to accomplish the following tasks:

Employee Interviews

During the execution of the search warrant, the interview team had been gathering information which can now be utilized by the environmental investigator. The results of these interviews should be thoroughly reviewed and a priority list of names established for those employees requiring a follow-up interview. In addition, information obtained by the records team regarding ex-employees and/or injured employees should also be added to the priority list.

During the interview process, it may be beneficial to the investigation to produce photographs, sketches, and Material Safety Data Sheets which were obtained during the execution of the search warrant. These may assist the employees in their descriptions of the various manufacturing processes and waste disposal procedures which took place at the facility.

Chemical Inventory Review

The chemical raw product suppliers should be contacted and interviewed. The environmental investigator should attempt to establish the amounts of raw hazardous chemical products shipped to the suspect facility. Once this information is obtained, it should be compared to the records of hazardous waste shipments made by the facility. In addition, the chemical supplier's procedures regarding Material Safety Data Sheets should be reviewed. The criminal investigator should attempt to determine if the MSDSs are shipped with each type of chemical and with each shipment of chemicals.

The salesperson for the chemical supplier should also be interviewed. He or she may have had direct conversations with individuals at the suspect facility regarding chemical product and chemical waste handling. This, along with the physical location of the MSDSs (i.e., whose desk they were found in) may help to establish *knowledge* on the part of an individual at the facility.

Analytical Evidence Review

The laboratory analysis of the chemical evidence removed from the facility during the search warrant should be compared with any known hazardous chemical raw product utilized by the facility. If methyl ethyl ketone and benzene were found in the chemical evidence analysis, it is essential that the criminal investigator also locate these chemicals in the hazardous raw chemical product purchased and utilized by the facility.

The chemical supplier's sales records, the chemical supplier's MSDS information, the facility's seized records of chemical purchases, the facility's seized MSDSs, chemical raw product analysis results, analysis results for suspected discharge points (i.e., pipes, pumps, sink traps) and analysis results for all suspected endpoints (i.e., storm drains, leaching pools, sewers) should be compared. By making this chemical-based comparison, the environmental investigator will be able to trace the various hazardous chemical products from their arrival into the facility, to their eventual release into the environment as a hazardous waste.

Interviewing the Suspect(s)

Those individuals suspected of being responsible for the hazardous waste discharges at the facility, should receive an in-depth interview (barring any Right-to-Counsel issues). Initial interviews may have been conducted by the search-warrant interview team. However, at this stage of the investigation, the environmental investigator should have a good working knowledge of the facility's manufacturing process and chemical-product handling procedures.

As in any other type of criminal investigation, the environmental investigator should be accompanied by another officer when interviewing suspects. The interview will have several purposes. First, the environmental investigator will make an attempt to gain new information regarding the illegal hazardous waste disposal at the facility. He or she will also attempt to corroborate existing evidence through admissions of guilt made by the suspect.

In many instances, the suspect will offer some form of explanation as to how the hazardous waste appeared in the storm drain or leaching pool. These explanations may include such defenses as "a former disgruntled employee did it," "a disgruntled neighbor did it," "a competitor did it," or "it was caused by an Act of God." Regardless of what the explanation is, the suspect will thereafter have to stand by this explanation throughout the duration of the case. The environmental investigator should accurately record these explanations. He or she must then investigate these explanations thoroughly.

Chapter 3

HAZARDOUS WASTE ABANDONMENT INVESTIGATIONS

Hazardous waste abandonment investigations offer a unique challenge to the environmental investigator. The most common form of this type of crime involves the abandonment of small containers and 55-gallon drums on the roadside or behind buildings. These crimes may also involve the abandonment of medical waste, asbestos, petroleum products, discharges from tankers and entire trailer loads of drums (see Figures 17 & 18). As with any other type of crime, the success of the investigation and prosecution may depend on the evidence-gathering procedures utilized at the crime scene. When approaching a hazardous waste abandonment crime scene, environmental investigators must recognize that *environmental crime is no different from any other crime, with the exception that the evidence you gather may kill you.*

Figure 17. These blood vials contain the AIDS and Hepatitis B Viruses. Over 10,000 were found at this environmental crime scene.

Figure 18. This is a typical hazardous waste abandonment crime scene involving 55-gallon drums.

Notification

One of the most difficult tasks that the environmental investigator will face is the establishment of a proper notification procedure for hazardous waste abandonment crimes. It is common for law enforcement authorities to learn of these incidents many hours or even days after the discovery of the hazardous waste. On occasion, the environmental investigator will learn that the hazardous waste has already been removed from the scene, by order of a regulatory agency, and is now at a Treatment, Storage or Disposal facility (TSDF). It is essential that the environmental investigator establish formal written procedures that will allow for the immediate notification of law enforcement authorities whenever abandoned hazardous waste has been discovered.

Unfortunately, proper and immediate notification will not guarantee the integrity of an environmental crime scene. Hazardous waste abandonment cases typically involve responses by such groups as volunteer firemen, civilian fire marshals, local hazardous material response team members, health officials and environmental regulatory agency personnel. Each of these individuals and agencies may have a specific function to perform at these types of environmental incidents and may not be aware of the need to preserve the integrity of the crime scene. However, with good education, training, and communications, each of these groups, in conjunction with law enforcement, will be able to accomplish its tasks successfully.

Once the environmental investigator has received notification of a hazardous waste abandonment scene, he or she must immediately request that the scene be sealed. Barring any *immediate* threat to life and/or property, the first-responders should treat the scene as a *crime scene* and restrict all entry until qualified criminal investigative personnel arrive. In addition, the environmental investigator should establish a procedure for the immediate notification of criminal investigative support personnel such as forensic chemists, sample team members and backup team personnel.

Arrival at the Crime Scene

Upon arrival at the crime scene, the environmental investigator should locate the individual in charge and gather as much information as possible regarding the incident. In many situations, the individual in charge will be the incident coordinator. The environmental investigator should obtain any information regarding the initial reporting of the incident, names of possible witnesses and a listing of those individuals who may have had physical contact with the crime scene. It may become necessary to obtain samples of these same individuals' footprints, fingerprints, and/or vehicle tire tracks. These samples can then be compared to any physical evidence left behind by the suspect(s). Any evidence identified as belonging to a first-responder can then be eliminated.

The first-responders may have conducted initial field tests on the chemical evidence (i.e., pH, L.E.L, radiological). If any initial field testing has been completed prior to the arrival of the environmental investigator, the results and methods must be obtained. The results of any initial field tests may help the environmental investigator determine the types of analysis that will eventually need to be conducted on the chemical evidence (see "Sampling for Criminal Evidence: Field Tests " in Chapter 5). In addition, the environmental investigator must determine if the initial field-testing methods caused any possible cross-contamination of the chemical evidence.

The successful gathering of criminal evidence at a hazardous waste abandonment crime scene will depend on the training and experience of those individuals involved. As with the *search-warrant team*, each team member must be properly trained and certified within their discipline.

The amount of personnel and equipment needed at a hazardous waste abandonment crime scene will depend on the volume and types of hazardous wastes involved. However, certain mandated minimum requirements for personnel and equipment must be observed (see "The Search-Warrant Team" in Chapter 2).

Crime-Scene Coordinator

This position is held by the primary environmental investigator assigned to the criminal investigation. The crime-scene coordinator and his or her partner should complete the following tasks:[27]
    a. Receive a full briefing from the on-scene incident coordinator.
    b. Interview all witnesses present at the crime scene.

c. Conduct a briefing of all team personnel prior to any evidence-gathering activities being conducted in the hot zone.

d. Control the paperwork at the crime scene.

e. Enter the hot zone and conduct a criminal investigation.

f. Conduct a *postsearch briefing* prior to the chemical evidence gathering operation.

g. Determine what types of analysis is to be done on the chemical evidence removed.

Safety Officer

A safety officer must be present during any chemical evidence gathering operation involving hazardous waste (see "The Search-Warrant team" in Chapter 2). All issues regarding personnel safety are the responsibility of the safety officer. The HazMat backup team, the medical team, and the decontamination team should report directly to the safety officer. This individual will also determine the level of personal protective equipment to be worn by those individuals entering any designated hot zone. In addition, the safety officer will determine what decontamination procedures are to be followed. The collection of chemical evidence should not begin without the safety officer's knowledge and approval. It is essential that the safety officer and crime-scene coordinator be in continuous communication with each other throughout all evidence-gathering activities.

Safety Team

The HazMat backup team acts as support and emergency rescue for the investigative team and the sample team working within the designated hot zone, confined space, or both. If the investigative team and/or sample team consists of two individuals working within one of the above described areas, there must be at least two individuals acting as their backup team.

Decontamination

Hazardous waste abandonment crime scenes may involve chemical, biological, and/or radiological hazards. An evaluation of these hazards may require that a predetermined decontamination procedure be followed by those individuals exiting a designated hot zone. The specific decontamination procedure, based upon the hazards involved, will be determined by the safety officer. This procedure may include a simple removal and bagging of contaminated clothing. However, it may be necessary for all personnel exiting the hot zone to go through a multiple wash-down procedure. This type of decontamination procedure may produce contaminated wastewater. It is recommended that this material be pumped into a recovery drum. The contaminated wastewater should then be sampled and arrangements made for its proper disposal.

Emergency Medical Assistance

Whether or not to have a HazMat-certified medical team at a hazardous waste abandonment crime scene will depend on several factors. The evaluation of the hazard(s) involved, the location of the nearest medical facility, and weather conditions will impact on this decision. However, if the chemical hazard(s) present at the crime scene require the use of fully encapsulated chemical suits (Level "A"), it is recommended that a HazMat-certified medical team be present during all evidence-gathering activities.

The Sample Team

This is the most difficult and dangerous activity conducted at any hazardous waste abandonment crime scene. The proper gathering of chemical evidence goes far beyond collecting liquid (or solid) samples and placing them into containers. These individuals must be concerned with such issues as personal safety, evidence cross-contamination, proper sampling methodology, and maintaining the chain-of-custody for the chemical evidence. The sample team should be fully briefed by the crime-scene coordinator as to which hazardous waste containers are to be sampled and what types of analyses that will be conducted on the chemical evidence.

Laboratory Team

Many jurisdictions may lack the resources necessary to have a laboratory team respond to a hazardous waste abandonment crime scene. It may be necessary for the environmental investigator to rely on the expertise of the sample team when dealing with such issues as equipment sterilization and the proper recording of sampling methodologies. However, if a Laboratory team is available, it should consist of at least one qualified forensic chemist. As in the *search-warrant team* situation, the laboratory team's responsibilities will begin long before they enter a hazardous waste abandonment crime scene. Each piece of equipment that is to be used for the gathering of chemical evidence must be thoroughly inspected and sterilized prior to it being utilized at the crime scene. A full record of the sterilization procedure should be maintained by the laboratory team. Once at the crime scene, the laboratory team will maintain a record of the samples that have been taken, what scientific field tests have been conducted, and the results of those tests. In addition, they will maintain a log of the sampling methodology utilized by the sample team. The laboratory team should maintain the integrity of the evidence by following procedures that will rule out any possibility of cross-contamination and/or outside contamination of the chemical evidence.

At the closure of the crime scene, this team will take custody of the chemical evidence and transport it to a laboratory or chemical evidence storage area. These individuals must be trained in the handling of criminal evidence and hazardous materials.

When conducting an investigation at a hazardous waste abandonment crime scene, it is recommended that a qualified individual be appointed site *science officer*. This individual may assist the environmental investigator in the identification of various chemical waste products. He or she may also assist the environmental investigator in determining the proper sampling and analytical methodologies required based upon any field-test results and in the identification of a particular chemical compound.

Gathering Evidence in the Hot Zone

Once all the personnel at the crime scene have been fully briefed and the safety protocols established, the crime-scene coordinator and his or her partner will enter the hot zone and commence the evidence gathering operation. To safely and efficiently complete this task, the environmental investigators must have the proper equipment with them when entering the hot zone. For a typical hazardous waste abandonment crime scene involving abandoned drums, this equipment should include:

• Appropriate chemical clothing based upon the suspected chemical hazard.

• Steel-toed, chemical-proof boots.

• Appropriate chemical gloves based upon the suspected chemical hazard.

• Several pairs of surgical gloves.

• A Self-Contained Breathing Apparatus with a full 60-minute air bottle.

• An aluminum (non-sparking) clipboard.

• A pen for crime-scene notes.

• A bold marker for filling in sample-point identification information on the sampling placards.

• Several preprinted placards for sample point identification.

• Duct tape, magnetic clips, or suction cup clips for attaching sampling placards to the hazardous waste containers.

• An L.E.L./O_2 meter for atmosphere flammability readings.

• A radiological meter capable of determining the presence of Alpha particles, Beta particles and/or Gamma rays.

• pH paper and pH chart.

• A waterproof auto-focus camera with sealed electronic flash.

• Evidence bags of assorted sizes.

• A beryllium (spark proof) bung wrench which is capable of opening various types of hazardous waste containers.

• A knife capable of cutting tape. This item should be taped to the calf of the environmental investigator and may be used under emergency conditions to cut away and remove a severely contaminated chemical suit.

• A fingerprint kit equipped with various dusting powders, brushes, and fingerprint lifting tape.

• A stethoscope for the audio monitoring of any container which appears to be swollen.

• Communication equipment which will allow for hands-free operation and direct communication with the safety officer and other individual working within the hot zone.

While inside the hot zone, the investigative team should attempt to complete the following evidence gathering tasks:

• Photograph the entire undisturbed crime scene from all angles.

• Complete a radiological survey of the entire crime scene.[28] The radiological survey should begin at the outermost perimeter, with continuous readings being made up to the surface areas of all hazardous waste containers.

• Complete a LEL reading to determine if any potentially flammable gases are present.[29]

• Determine if the material has been spilled or is leaking from the hazard waste containers.

• Determine if any of the hazardous waste containers appear to be swollen. This may be an indication that the material inside the containers may be under extreme pressure.

• Determine if any of the hazardous waste containers are emitting noise. Such noises may be *pings* or *pops.* These sounds may be spaced several seconds apart. If they should become more rapid, the hot zone should be *evacuated immediately.* This may be an indication that the metal container is stretching due to extreme interior pressure and that the container may be on the verge of catastrophic failure. This audio examination may be accomplished through the use of a stethoscope. Any interior container noise should be reported to the safety officer immediately.

• Determine if there are any signs of waste crystallization. This may be indicative of explosive peroxides or sodium cyanide. Any signs of product crystallization should be reported to the safety officer immediately.

• Note, photograph, and cast any footprints and/or tire tracks present.

• Note, photograph and lift any fingerprints on the hazardous waste containers. Special attention should be paid the to bottom surfaces of any drums and/or cans. These are the natural gripping areas used to lift these types of containers. If the suspect(s) lifted these containers without gloves, the bottom surfaces will be the most likely areas in which fingerprints may be found.

• Photograph and record any US Department of Transportation information on the drums.

• Photograph and record all other markings on the hazardous waste containers.

• Photograph and record all label information on the containers. If the label is legible and can be removed intact, it should be recovered and placed into an evidence bag. Many labels may have illegible, yet potentially valuable, information on them. If they cannot be removed intact, the metal area surrounding the label should be carefully cut out after the chemical evidence has been removed. This procedure will require that the hazardous waste be transferred into a recovery drum. It may also require numerous rinses which will produce contaminated waste water. It is essential that this contaminated waste water be contained and disposed of properly. This type of evidence recovery is difficult and should be done only under the supervision of qualified chemists and hazardous material trained personnel. In addition, every effort should be made to identify the chemical waste and its characteristics prior to attempting this type of evidence recovery. At the completion of this operation, the cut piece of metal and the attached illegible label should be sent to the documents department of a crime lab. Information on faded labels may be raised using document enhancement techniques, such as infrared and infrared fluorescence (see Figures 19 & 20).

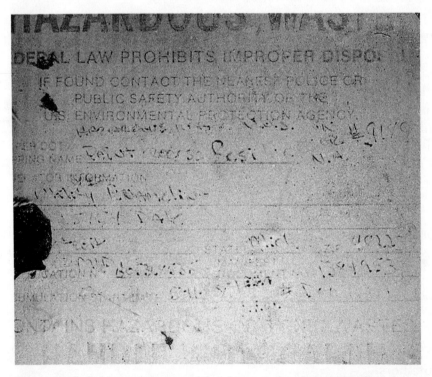

Figure 19. Faded hazardous waste label from an abandoned 55-gallon drum. This drum was one of 115 drums that were abandoned in a suburban area.

Figure 20. The document section of the crime lab was able to enhance an area of the label shown in Figure 19. These numbers represent a partial EPA Hazardous Waste Generator Identification number.

• The surrounding ground area should be carefully searched for any other form of physical evidence. Any closed hazardous waste containers should be lifted and/or tilted so that their undersides, and the ground area underneath the containers, may be examined for possible physical evidence.

• A sketch should be made of the entire crime scene including the position and location of each hazardous waste container. The crime scene sketch should also include the location of any other physical evidence recovered.

• The investigative team should open each drum and repeat the LEL and radiological tests. The LEL reading should be taken directly over the exposed hazardous waste. This will assist the environmental investigator in determining if any flammable vapors are being produced by the hazardous waste. A radiological reading should be taken directly over the exposed hazardous waste. Radioactive Alpha particles and Beta particles may be shielded by the plastic or metal which makes up the hazardous waste container's construction.

• If the hazardous waste containers have removable lids, the lids should be removed and the interiors of the containers examined. The interiors of these containers may contain other physical evidence, such as trash and smaller containers.

• A field pH test should be conducted on the hazardous waste. This field test may assist the environmental investigator in determining the types of chemical analysis which will be needed to further the investigation (see "Sampling for Criminal Evidence: Field Tests" in Chapter 5).

• The hazardous waste should be physically examined through the use of a *Coliwasa Tube* (see Figure 21). This will supply a visual perspective of the waste column and may assist the environmental investigator in determining analytical needs.

Figure 21. Environmental investigators examining the hazardous waste
column prior to sampling.

• Each hazardous waste container that has been selected for sampling should be placarded and photographed. The sampling placard should contain, at a minimum, agency information, the current date, and the field sample number.

Postsearch Briefing

After exiting the hot zone, the environmental investigators must meet with the sample team, HazMat backup team, science officer, and safety officer.[30] During this postsearch briefing, the site hazards, sampling protocols, sampling parameters, and analytical requirements will be discussed.

In most instances, the chemical evidence gathering operation will be the only opportunity to gather chemical evidence. Normally, at the conclusion of a hazardous waste abandonment crime scene, the hazardous waste is removed by a licensed hazardous waste transporter. It is then taken to a facility for safe treatment and/or eventual disposal. Due to the limited amount of time that the chemical evidence is available, it is essential that the proper analytical requirements be determined at the crime scene. All of the available information must be evaluated in making the determination as to what types of analyses will be required to further the investigation and meet the requirements of any criminal statutes. The environmental investigator may require analyses for metals, volatile organic compounds, flammable liquids, acids, caustics, pesticides, herbicides, and other compounds which may fall under the regulations and/or criminal statutes which were violated by abandonment of the hazardous waste.

Chemical Evidence Gathering

This is the most critical part of the evidence gathering at a hazardous waste abandonment crime scene. Due to the complexities involved with chemical evidence gathering, the potential for error is extremely high. The crime-scene coordinator, safety officer, and site science officer should, if possible, witness the sampling operation from outside the hot zone. Through the use of radio communication, simple reminders and corrections can be relayed to the sample team if necessary. In addition, the sample team may identify evidence overlooked by the Investigative team and may determine that additional analytical parameters are required.

The sample team should also determine the volume of material present in each hazardous waste container sampled. Each measurement should correspond to a particular sample point (i.e., Field Sample # 1SD 3/21/97 = 27 inches of liquid). A full description of the hazardous waste container(s) and a record of any hazardous waste measurements made by the sample team should be maintained by the crime-scene coordinator (see "Sampling for Criminal Evidence: Volume Reading Techniques" in Chapter 5).

At the completion of all evidence gathering activities, the chemical evidence should be properly sealed, stored, and transported to a laboratory or chemical evidence holding area. A proper chain-of-custody must be maintained at all times.

Abandoned Trailer Investigations

Hazardous waste abandonment crime scenes may involve large volumes of hazardous waste. In some instances, these investigations will involve abandoned trailer loads of hazardous waste drums and assorted hazardous waste containers. Abandoned trailers such as these may have been stolen and/or have had all possible ownership identifiers removed.

The proper investigation of this type of hazardous waste abandonment crime scene requires time, patience and planning on the part of the environmental investigator. If there is no *immediate* danger to the community and/or the environment, it may be in the best interest of the investigation to secure, seal, and store the trailer until the necessary resources and off-loading facilities can be obtained.

Trailer Exterior

The trailer exterior, including the undercarriage, should be thoroughly examined by the environmental investigator. All obvious identifiers should be noted and eventually traced. In addition, air line and electrical line connection points should be examined for fingerprints. The interior and exterior door surfaces, at all levels, should also be examined for fingerprints.

Off-Loading Operation

There are several different techniques which may be utilized when off loading hazardous waste containers from a trailer. One technique involves the use of a dual loading bay and an empty trailer. By placing the empty trailer in the bay next to the trailer containing the hazardous waste, the environmental investigator will be able to examine and sample each container as it is brought out. The hazardous waste containers may be removed by a *drum dolly* or a specially fitted forklift. After examination and sampling for chemical evidence, the hazardous waste containers may be placed onto the empty trailer. Another method is to remove the hazardous waste containers and place them in a secure hazardous waste storage area (see Figure 22). The hazardous waste containers may be examined and sampled prior to being placed into the storage area. Regardless of the method used, it is essential that all safety regulations, including confined space regulations, be followed carefully. This type of operation may require the continuous air monitoring of the trailer's interior atmosphere. Once the trailer has been completely unloaded, the interior should be carefully examined for fingerprints, discarded tools, documents, trash and any other physical evidence which may be present.

Figure 22. An abandoned trailer filled with hazardous waste drums is carefully off-loaded. Each drum is examined for physical evidence.

Hazardous Waste Tanker Investigations

Many criminal environmental investigations will involve tanker trucks containing hazardous waste. These cases may involve the illegal transport, storage, and/or discharge of hazardous waste. When a tanker truck is suspected of having been used to discharge hazardous waste, a search warrant may be required before any chemical evidence can be removed from the tanker or before the cab of the vehicle can be searched for documentary evidence. If a search warrant is required, there are several preliminary investigative steps which can be taken in an effort to gather the probable cause necessary for the obtaining of the warrant. These steps include the following:

Driver Interview

This is the best source of information regarding the activities for which the tanker truck was used. The driver may be cooperative and may supply information regarding the material in the tanker. He or she may supply information regarding the source of the hazardous waste (e.g., point of generation). In some cases, the driver may even supply his or her consent to have the vehicle searched and chemical samples seized as evidence. However, he or she may be uncooperative, which will require that the environmental investigator take further steps.

Manifests and Permits

If the driver cannot or will not produce a proper hazardous waste transportation permit and/or a hazardous waste manifest, the environmental investigator should note this and place this information in his or her search warrant application.

Placards

The U.S. Department of Transportation requires that vehicles transporting hazardous wastes bear placards.[31] The lack of placards on a tanker or the presence of the wrong placards (based upon field tests) may be seen as evidence of an effort to mislead law enforcement and/or regulatory agency officials as to the tanker's contents. Lack of proper placards on the tanker should be noted by the environmental investigator and should be used as part of the probable cause necessary for obtaining a search warrant.

Field Tests

In many jurisdictions, the results of the field tests used to protect the safety of the investigative entry team may also be used to establish probable cause. Meter readings for flammable vapors, radiological meter readings, and pH tests can all be conducted without removing a chemical sample from the tanker. These safety tests can be conducted on exterior surfaces, ports, exposed hoses, and/or on any leaks or ground discharges. While the primary purpose of these types of field tests is to protect the health and safety of those at the crime scene, the results may indicate the presence of some form of hazardous material or hazardous waste (see "Sampling for Criminal Evidence: Field Tests" in Chapter 5).

Tanker Discharges

If the tanker is discharging its contents, it is vital that the position of any switches or valves be noted. Today, many tanker trucks have the dual ability to vacuum material as well as discharge material. By noting the position of all switches and valves, the environmental investigator will be able to prove that the tanker was discharging material and not removing it. In addition, the tanker's manufacturer will be able to supply the environmental investigator with information regarding the tanker's discharge capabilities (e.g., gallons per minute). This information, combined with a known length of discharge time will help determine the actual amount of material discharged from the tanker (see Figure 23).

Figure 23. This tanker was seized while discharging its contents into a river.
The discharge was timed and later compared to the discharge flow rate of the tanker.

Chapter 4

DRUM-TRACING TECHNIQUES

When tracing hazardous waste drums, the environmental investigator has five distinct areas of inquiry which he or she may pursue in an attempt to identify the suspect(s). These areas include the vehicle used to transport the hazardous waste, the person or persons who abandoned the hazardous waste, other physical evidence found at the crime scene, the container, and the chemical analysis of the hazardous waste. By pursuing each of these areas, the environmental investigator may be able to develop the information necessary to identify the suspect(s).

Vehicle

The abandonment of hazardous waste containers normally involves the use of some form of motor vehicle to transport the material to the abandonment site. In attempting to identify this vehicle, the environmental investigator should take the following steps:

Witnesses

The area in which the material was abandoned should be canvassed for witnesses. This may involve interviewing local residents and business owners. If an approximate disposal time can be determined, the environmental investigator should return to the abandonment scene on several different days (or nights), at the approximate disposal time. Any individuals traveling through this area should be stopped and interviewed.

Tire Tracks

As discussed earlier, all tire tracks should be measured, photographed and cast. If the type and size of the tire can be determined, the environmental investigator may be able to identify the types of vehicles that utilize that particular model of tire.

Vehicle Size

Even without the aid of tire-track identification, information regarding the approximate size of the vehicle may be determined by the weight and volume of the hazardous waste. Depending on the actual density of the waste, one 55-gallon drum may weigh anywhere between 300 and 650 pounds (i.e., chemical density of 1.4 = 11.676 lb. per gallon x 55 gallons = 642.18 lb. per drum). Ten full drums of hazardous waste may weigh between 3,000 and 6,420 pounds. The laboratory utilized for the hazardous waste analysis will be able to provide the various densities for the chemical samples removed during the evidence-gathering operation. In addition, ten upright drums of hazardous waste will take up approximately 35 square feet of space (i.e., drum diameter = 1.875 ft.; 1.875^2 = 3.51 sq. ft. x 10 drums = 35.1 sq. ft.). In this case, the environmental investigator will know that, based upon a chemical density of 1.4, with a total of ten 55 gallon drums, he or she will be searching for a vehicle that can carry 6,420 pounds, with a storage capacity of at least 35 square feet. The drum weights and drum volumes should assist the environmental investigator in narrowing the list of possible vehicle models used in the crime.

In addition to the above, a careful examination of the environmental crime scene may determine whether or not a vehicle lift gate was used to unload the hazardous waste drums. Many trucks come equipped with a lift that will allow the drums to be slowly lowered to the ground. Marks and/or indentations on the surface of the ground made by the weight of the drums and marks left behind by a lift gate resting on the ground may indicate the use of such a device. If it is suspected that the vehicle was equipped with such a lift gate device, it will further narrow the list of possible vehicle models used to transport the hazardous waste to the crime scene.

Vehicle Contamination

If a lift gate was not used and the hazardous waste drums were dumped off the back of a vehicle, some hazardous waste spillage may have occurred. This may be caused by loose bungs and/or drum lids. It may also be caused if the drums rupture upon hitting the ground. When this type of spillage occurs, some interior and/or exterior vehicle contamination may result. If this is the case and the suspect vehicle is eventually located, trace chemical samples from the suspect vehicle can be compared with the sample analysis conducted on the hazardous waste at the crime scene.

In addition to the chemical analysis comparisons, the environmental investigator should note that hazardous waste contamination, due to spillage, may leave behind a distinctive odor. Many solvents, herbicides and pesticides will seep into the walls and floor of the vehicle and may leave a distinctive odor. This distinctive odor may last for several days or weeks (see Figure 24). When a suspected vehicle has been located and spillage is suspected, the vehicle should be checked for chemical odors.

Figure 24. This vehicle was used to dump 15 drums of pesticide waste. When the vehicle was located, a heavy odor of pesticides was noted. The wood floor was then sampled for traces of pesticides

Person or Persons

As with any other type of crime, the person or persons committing the environmental crime may have left behind physical evidence which may lead the environmental investigator to their eventual identification. Clearly, the most valuable identifier is fingerprints left behind by the suspect(s). As stated earlier, particular attention should be paid to the edges and bottoms of containers. These are the areas where hands are naturally placed when moving or lifting containers. However, on many occasions fingerprints will not be found on the hazardous waste drums. They may, however, be found on discarded empty cans, bottles, tools, cellophane wrappers, and the interior of chemical gloves utilized by the suspect(s). In addition, any footprints left behind by the suspect(s) will assist the environmental investigator in the identification process. Shoe size and type of shoe worn by the suspect(s) may assist the environmental investigator at some future point in the investigation.

Other Physical Evidence

When hazardous waste drums are abandoned, perpetrators have a tendency to abandon other items along with the waste. Items such as cash register receipts, shopping bags, computer printouts, invoices, hand tools, and old pumps may also be found at the scene. Any of these items might supply information useful in identifying the suspect(s). It should also be noted that many of these items may be found in the interior of the drums (see Figure 25). Any drums with removable tops should have their interiors' inspected for other physical evidence. Any documents found inside the drums should be carefully packaged for future examination. These packages should also be clearly marked so that document examiners are aware of the possibility of hazardous waste contamination.

Check these additional features
only with Child Safe Safety Surface:

Figure 25. This document, found floating in the hazardous waste, led to the eventual identification and conviction of the suspect.

Container

Information found on the exterior of the drums will come in many different forms. Information found on labels, writing on the drums and Department of Transportation information may all assist the environmental investigator in locating the suspect(s).

Labels

As indicated earlier, labels should be recorded, photographed, and removed whenever possible. Information regarding the original manufacturer, lot numbers, and the type of chemical product may be listed on the label. If this information is present, the chemical manufacturer should be contacted and a list of customers obtained. By limiting the inquiry to a specific geographical area, the environmental investigator will be able to obtain a list of the product users within his or her area. These product users can then be checked for hazardous waste shipments and past regulatory agency inspections.

If the only information remaining on the label is the product name the OPD Chemical Buyers Directory (see "Search Warrants:

Developing Probable Cause" in Chapter 2) will supply the environmental investigator with a list of companies that manufacture that particular product. Each company will be likely to use a different label. By supplying these companies with photographs of the labels recovered at the environmental crime scene, the actual chemical supplier may be identified and a local customer list obtained.

Writing on the Drums

Handwritten information on drums may be of great value to the environmental investigator. Similar number codes and word patterns found at different crime scenes may link those crime scenes (see Figures 26 & 27). In addition, a handwritten sequential numbering system found on the drums may be indicative of a prior environmental survey.

Figure 26. This writing linked 5 different crime scenes, involving 35 drums of hazardous waste. It eventually led to an operating clandestine cocaine laboratory.

Figure 27. This is one of 115 drums of hazardous waste which were abandoned on a stolen trailer. The sequential numbering system on the drums suggests a prior environmental survey and the possible existence of laboratory reports.

If the suspect hired a private environmental company to inventory and classify the waste, it would be a standard industry practice for the company to number the drums sequentially for chemical sample identification purposes. Once the sample analysis was completed, a copy of the results and the cost of disposal would normally be given to the suspect. This supplies the environmental investigator with two important elements of the crime. These elements are *knowledge* and *motive.* The laboratory analysis supplies the *knowledge* as to the existence of the hazardous waste. The fact that the generator received a price for legal disposal and then abandoned the hazardous waste is indicative of a financial *motive* for committing the crime.

Department of Transportation Information

The environmental investigator will frequently find U.S. Department of Transportation (DOT) information stenciled on the sides of drums (see Figure 28). It is also common to find this information on small labels. The U.S. Department of Transportation requires the manufacturers of drums to place certain data on the drums prior to them being filled with a hazardous material.[32]

Figure 28. This is the information the U.S. Department of Transportation requires to be printed on chemical drums.

The information in Figure 28 is interpreted as follows:
• UN = UNITED NATIONS.
• 1A2 = 1 (DRUM), A (STEEL), 2 (OPEN HEAD).
• Y= PACKAGING FOR GROUP II & III TESTS.
• 1.2 = SPECIFIC GRAVITY OR MASS FOR PACKAGE DESIGN.
• 100 = PRESURE TEST IN KILO PACALS (HYDROSTATIC TEST).
• 5/96 = MONTH & YEAR OF DRUM MANUFACTURE.
• US = COUNTRY OF ORIGIN.
• M4709 = CODE FOR NAME AND ADDRESS OR SYMBOL OF DRUM MANUFACTURER.

The two most important pieces of information listed above are the month/year of the drum's manufacture and the code which lists the name and address of the drum manufacturer. These two items alone may assist the environmental investigator in both isolating and eliminating suspects.

The month and year of the drum's manufacture, or "DOT date," is vital for the simple fact that it eliminates suspects. When the original chemical supplier and chemical name are known, the environmental investigator may limit his or her list of suspects to those companies that purchased that particular chemical product after the printed DOT date found on the container. Any company that has made its only purchase(s) of that particular chemical product, prior to the DOT date, is eliminated as a suspect.

The code listing the drum manufacturer's name and address can also assist the environmental investigator. Many drums are manufactured with particular color schemes (e.g., blue drums with yellow tops). A chemical manufacturer may order only one drum color scheme from the drum manufacturer. Once the drum manufacturer has been located, they should be shown a photograph of the suspect hazardous waste drum. If there are any distinguishing features on the drum (e.g., color scheme and DOT date), the drum manufacturer may be able to identify the raw chemical product manufacturer that purchased the drum.

The names and addresses of drum manufacturers are listed by their code numbers in a DOT database in Washington, D.C. A copy of this database can be obtained by contacting the U.S. Department of Transportation, Hazardous Material Administrator, Washington, D.C.

The Chemical Analysis

Proper chemical analysis of the hazardous waste and a visual examination of the chemical sample itself may assist the environmental investigator in narrowing the list of suspected generators. It is vital that the proper laboratory analysis be completed for this type of forensic chemical evidence to be useful to the investigation. It will be of no forensic value to the environmental investigator to learn only that the waste failed an Ignitability Test or that the waste passed the TCLP test (see " Chemical Analysis of Criminal Evidence: Method Choice" in Chapter 6). Only a complete chemical analysis can assist the environmental investigator in identifying the suspect.

Experience will tell the environmental investigator which chemicals are used in the various types of industries. Chemicals such as sodium hydroxide, chromic acid, and cyanide are commonly found in the plating industry. The chemicals toluene, tetrachloroethylene, and acetone, when used together, are indicative of a clandestine cocaine processing laboratory, while tetrachloroethylene by itself is used in the dry-cleaning industry. The presence of the chemical methyl ethyl ketone by itself may not be of great value to the environmental investigator, but if he or she were to physically examine the sample and find small paint chips or flakes in the sample container, it may indicate that the generator is in the business of automobile collision repair.

As a general rule, the more unique the chemical is, the greater the possibility of locating the suspect. Unique chemicals and unique chemical combinations may only be produced by a handful of chemical manufacturers. This fact, combined with any information obtained regarding the original drum manufacturer's sales records, may greatly reduce the list of possible chemical manufacturers.

Chapter 5

SAMPLING FOR CRIMINAL EVIDENCE

The proper collection of samples at environmental crime scenes requires preparation and planning. The proper selection and preparation of sampling equipment, methods of sample collection, types of analyses required, site contamination control, chain-of-custody, and evidence storage are all critical to a successful investigation and prosecution. The environmental investigator has a responsibility to insure that the chemical evidence is collected and maintained properly. To fulfill this responsibility, one must have adequate knowledge with regard to the accepted sampling protocols and analytical methods approved by local, state, or federal agencies.

The purpose of this chapter is to acquaint the environmental investigator with a few of the approved equipment-preparation and sampling protocols utilized in evidence collection, specifically the methods and protocols described in the U.S. Environmental Protection Agency's "*Test Methods for Evaluating Solid Waste*" (SW 846).[33] These methods and protocols are intended to supply information regarding sampling and analysis as they are "related to compliance with RCRA [The Resource Conservation and Recovery Act of 1974] regulations."[34] In addition, SW 846 recommends that the information contained therein be used as a "guidance rather than in a step-by-step, word-by-word fashion."[35] However, it is imperative that the environmental investigator review all sampling regulations and/or requirements within his or her own state or locality.

Sampling Plan

This book has focused primarily on two types of environmental investigations in which sampling for criminal evidence may be required. The first type of investigation is that involving the environmental search warrant. In these situations the actual sample types and sample locations may not be known until after the search has been completed. In this case the sample plan will be set during the post-search briefing (see " Search Warrants: The Warrant Execution, Post-Search Briefing" in Chapter 2). The second type of investigation is that which deals with the abandonment of the hazardous waste. In this type of case, the crime scene must be completely examined and other types of evidence removed, prior to the commencement of any sampling operation. In hazardous waste abandonment investigations, the sampling plan will also be set at the post-search briefing (see "Hazardous waste Abandonment Investigations: Postsearch Briefing" in Chapter 3).

SW 846 states that "the primary objectives of a sampling plan for a solid waste (includes hazardous waste) are twofold: namely, to collect samples that will allow measurements of the chemical properties of the waste that are both accurate and precise."[36] In order to insure that this objective is met, the environmental investigator must meet with the other members of the team and develop a sampling plan that will provide the criminal evidence necessary to further the investigation and, at the same time, satisfy the sample collection criteria of the approved analytical method used for the analysis of the evidence.

The sampling plan will generally indicate the types of chemical analysis required (based upon prior knowledge of the waste stream and/or information developed during the search), sample point location, sampling equipment requirements, cross-contamination and outside contamination control samples, chain-of-custody procedures, personal protective equipment, and other safety issues.

Sample Bottle Identification and Preparation

There are numerous types of sample collection containers available today. The sample containers listed below are those commonly used for the collection of chemical evidence at environmental crime scenes. The following selection is by no means an all-inclusive list. However, each sampling container, regardless of its intended use, will require some form of preparation prior to utilization. Even *new* sample containers may not meet the preparation requirements listed in SW 846.

The environmental investigator must insure that the proper preparation procedures have been followed, prior to any evidence-gathering operation. In addition, he or she must insure that documentation exists which clearly indicates the name of the individual who prepared the sampling containers, the methodology used, and the date on which they were prepared. Court challenges based on possible sample contamination due to preexisting container contamination will be prevented by documenting and utilizing the proper preparation procedures.

Volatile Organic Compound Bottle

The sampling containers used for volatile organic compound collection are standard 40 ml glass, screw-cap bottles with Teflon-lined silicon septa. These sampling containers may be used for both liquids and solids. The vials and septa should be washed with a detergent, rinsed with tap and distilled water, and dried in an oven for 1 hour at 105°C before use.[37]

Semivolatile Organic Compound Bottle

The sampling containers used for collecting semivolatile organic compounds (including herbicides and pesticides) should be composed of glass or Teflon and have screw-caps with Teflon-lined septa. The vials should be washed with detergent, rinsed with tap water, rinsed with distilled water, and then rinsed with methanol (or isopropanol).[38]

Inorganic Compound Bottle

The sampling containers used for inorganic compounds (including total metals and T.C.L.P metals) should be composed of linear polyethylene, polypropylene, borosilicate glass, or Teflon. The containers should be prepared using the following steps: detergent wash, tap water rinse, 1:1 nitric acid rinse, tap water rinse, 1:1 hydrochloric acid rinse, tap-water rinse and a metal-free water rinse.[39]

Ignitability Bottle

Sampling containers used for the determination of ignitability should be standard glass, screw-cap bottles, with Teflon-lined silicon septa's. These sample containers may be used for both liquids and solids. The vials and septa should be washed with a detergent, rinsed with tap water and distilled water, and dried in an oven for 1 hour at 105°C before use.

Cyanide Bottle

Cyanide samples may be collected in glass or plastic bottles. These containers should be cleaned and rinsed thoroughly.[40]

Oil and Grease/Total Petroleum Hydrocarbons Bottle

These sample collection containers should be made of glass, approximately 1 liter in size, with a PTFE-lined screw-cap. The sampling containers should be prepared by using a detergent wash, tap-water rinse, and baked at 200-250°C for a minimum of 1 hour. After cooling, the mouth of the bottle should be covered with aluminum foil and a screw-cap placed onto the bottle. A solvent wash may be used in place of baking.[41]

Phenols and Polychlorinated Biphenyl Bottle

Sampling containers used for determining phenols and polychlorinated biphenyls should be standard glass, screw-cap bottles, with Teflon-lined silicon septa. The vials and septa should be washed with a detergent, rinsed with distilled or deionized water, and dried in an oven at 105°C for approximately 1 hour.

Sample Device Identification and Preparation

The sampling devices listed below are just a few of the items which may be used for chemical evidence collection at an environmental crime scene. Each sampling device listed below has a specific use depending upon the location and type of the material being sampled.

- Coliwasa Tube
- Extension Auger
- Ponar Grab Sampler

- Weighted Sampler
- Dipper
- Bailer

- Shovels
- Spoons
- Back hoe

Ideally, a separate sampling device should be prepared for each sample point. The preparation should be based upon the analysis method that will be utilized in the laboratory. However, this would require the purchase and preparation of numerous duplicate items. While coliwasa tubes may be inexpensive and disposable, other sampling devices such as stainless steel extension augers and Ponar grab samplers are not. Normally, only one or two of these expensive sampling devices would be available to the environmentally investigator at a crime scene. Therefore, in order to maintain the integrity of the chemical evidence, it may become necessary to clean and prepare, for reuse, certain sampling devices while at the environmental crime scene. The integrity of the chemical evidence may be maintained by basic cleaning and preparation techniques. This includes the washing of the sampling device with a detergent. The device should then be rinsed with tap water and then rinsed again with distilled water.

Types of Analysis

Perhaps the most difficult decision facing the environmental investigator at an environmental crime scene is choosing the correct analysis to be performed on the chemical evidence about to be seized. Due to the different sampling container requirements described above, these decisions must normally be made *before* any chemical evidence is gathered.

Many factors must be taken into account when making this decision. These factors include the type of industry, the physical appearance of the waste product, information developed at the scene, and any statutory requirements which may exist. The environmental investigator must know exactly what needs to be proven under the applicable statute and which chemical analyses should be employed. This should be accomplished by determining what is required by the criminal statute(s) and what is needed to further the investigation (e.g., trace amounts of chemicals found for forensic connections). The following is a list of some of the more common analytical parameters which may be tested at an environmental crime scene:

- Volatile Organic Compounds
- Semi-Volatile Organic Compounds

- Metals Analysis
- Total Characteristic Leaching Procedure

- EP Toxicity
- Total Petroleum Hydrocarbons

- Cyanide
- Polychlorinated Biphenyls

- Ignitability
- pH

- Radiation
- Asbestos

- Corrosivity
- Fecal Coliform

Field Tests

The utilization of field tests, at an environmental crime scene, will assist the environmental investigator in determining the investigation's analytical needs. These field tests should be completely documented, indicating the type of test, equipment utilized, test results, and the name of the individual conducting the test. The following is a partial listing of the various field tests which may be utilized at an environmental crime scene:

pH

This simple field test will help determine the presence of acids or caustics. In addition, if the environmental investigator suspects the presence of plating waste, a high pH may be indicative of the presence of cyanide.

LEL/O²

LEL (Lower Explosive Limit) and O² (Oxygen) meters are essential equipment at any environmental crime scene. The LEL meter, when placed over a sampling point, will produce a scaled, positive reading if flammable substances are present in the air. A positive reading on this device may indicate to the environmental investigator that a sample should be collected and subjected to an ignitability test in the laboratory.

The O² meter will indicate how much oxygen is present in the atmosphere. A lower than normal reading may indicate that an unknown substance has displaced the oxygen. This is especially useful in confined areas where the discharge of hazardous waste is suspected. It is also of critical importance to the safety of the sampling team and may dictate whether self-contained breathing apparatus will be required.

Radiological

The Geiger counter is one of the best instruments to use when the presence of radioactive material is suspected. However, there are several different types of Geiger counters available today. Some Geiger counters may measure only gamma rays and beta particles. While others will only measure alpha particles. It addition, some Geiger counters are designed to read only high levels of radiation. A negative reading on a meter such as this may be misleading. Lower levels of radiation may still be present at a level below the detection limit of the Geiger counter being used. As with all field testing equipment, the capabilities and limitations of the instrument must be fully understood by the environmental investigator.

Flame Ionization Detection (FID)

The flame ionization detector detects the presence of organic compounds by using a hydrogen/air flame. Ions are produced when small amounts of certain organic chemicals are introduced into the hydrogen/air flame. The positive ions produced move toward a negatively-charged collector, producing an electrical current which is proportional to the amount of the organic compound entering the flame. This small electrical current is electronically amplified and is then sent to the readout screen. This device has a wide range and is highly sensitive to hydrocarbon vapors. This device can be described as an electronic bloodhound. It has the ability to backtrack certain hydrocarbons and chlorinated hydrocarbons to their concentrated point-of-origin.

Photo-ionization Detection (PID)

The photo-ionization detector consists of an ultraviolet lamp and an ionization chamber. If an organic compound enters the ionization chamber and has an ionization potential below the energy level of the light from the ultraviolet lamp, that organic compound will break apart into a positively charged ion and an electron. This process is called photo-ionization. The ions produced are accelerated to a collecting electrode and produce an electrical current. The amount of current produced is proportional to the amount of organic compound present. The PID is very sensitive to aromatic compounds, some chlorinated compounds and a limited amount of inorganic compounds such as nitric oxide and ammonia. As with the FID, this instrument is useful in determining contaminated areas and discharge points-of-origin.

X-ray Fluorescent Detection

The x-ray fluorescent detector is useful in determining the presence of certain metals. This device contains it own radiological source that is capable of exciting such metals as chromium, cadmium and lead causing them to emit x-rays. This device can determine what metal (qualitative) is present by the amount of energy in the x-rays that are emitted. The concentration of a metal present (quantitative) is determined by measuring the intensity of the x-rays being emitted by each metal. These instruments may be quite accurate and can produce on-screen results in the parts per million (ppm) range.

Dräeger Tubes

The Dräeger-Tube detection system utilizes tubes packed with an indicating substance that reacts with a specific contaminant being drawn through the tube and develops a visible color as a result of the reaction. Air samples are drawn through individual tubes by use of an air pump. The color of the tube is then checked for a positive or negative reading. In certain instances, if the contaminant is known, and in a concentration that can be detected, the Dräeger-Tubes can be used to give a semi-quantitative result. There are several hundred different substances that may be individually identified through the use of this system. Unfortunately, there are thousands of hazardous chemicals and chemical mixtures used in industry today. The Dräeger-Tube system can detect only a limited percentage of these chemicals. In addition, most of the Dräeger Tubes have a limited shelf life and are capable of only being used once. This may present some problems at an environmental crime scene involving multiple suspected areas of contamination. When complex chemical mixtures are present, such as those found in some hazardous wastes, it is recommended that the Dräeger-Tube system be replaced with direct air sampling, which utilizes adsorbent tubes for sample collection.

Documentation

In addition to the chain-of-custody requirements which are discussed later, there are, at a minimum, 20 separate pieces of information, that should be recorded for each sample point. An environmental crime scene that produces 20 sample points may require several hundred separate notations in the crime-scene records. The following is a listing of notations which should be recorded:

• Sample Number	• Date	• Case Number	• Location
• Sample Point Description	• Vessel Dimensions	• Volume of Waste	• Name of Person Taking Measurements
• Sample Time	• Lead Sampler	• Assistant Sampler	• Sample Matrix

- Analysis   • Name of   • Type of   • Label
  Requested   Photographer   Photography   Information
                                                                  (Drums)

- DOT   • Label   • Equipment   • Name of
  Information   Location   Decontamination   Note Taker
  (Drums)   (Drums)

To better maintain and organize this amount of data, it is suggested that a preprinted form be used for each sample point at an environmental crime scene (see Figures 29 & 30).

(FRONT)
SAMPLE POINT SHEET

SAMPLE#_____ DATE:___/___/___ CASE#_____

INCIDENT LOCATION:_____

_____

****

SAMPLE POINT LOCATION:_____

_____

SAMPLE POINT DISCRIPTION: 55 GAL. DRUM   30 GAL. DRUM   5 GAL. CAN

LEACHING POOL   STORM DRAIN   GROUND   AIR   TANKER

SEPTIC TANK   ABOVE GROUND TANK   BELOW GROUND TANK

PIPE   HOSE   PUMP   OTHER:_____
****

RELATIVE MEASUREMENTS

VESSEL DIMENSIONS: HEIGHT:_____WIDTH:_____DEPTH:_____

LIQUID - SLUDGE - SOLID DEPTH: FEET:_____INCHES:_____

MEASUREMENTS TAKEN BY:_____
****

TIME SAMPLE TAKEN:_____AM PM

SAMPLER:_____ASS'T. SAMPLER_____
****
SAMPLE TYPE: SOLID LIQUID   SLUDGE   AIR   GAS

ANALYSIS: VOLATILE   SEMI VOLATILE   METALS TCLP   PHENOLS   FLASHPOINT

pH   PCB   TPH FECAL COLIFORM   ASBESTOS   CYANIDE   RADIOLOGICAL

OTHER:_____
****

PHOTOS BY:_____35MM   VIDEO   POLAROID OTHER:_____

ABOVE RECORDED BY:_____
****

Figure 29. The preprinted Sample Point Form will allow for the orderly and standardized recording of sampling data.

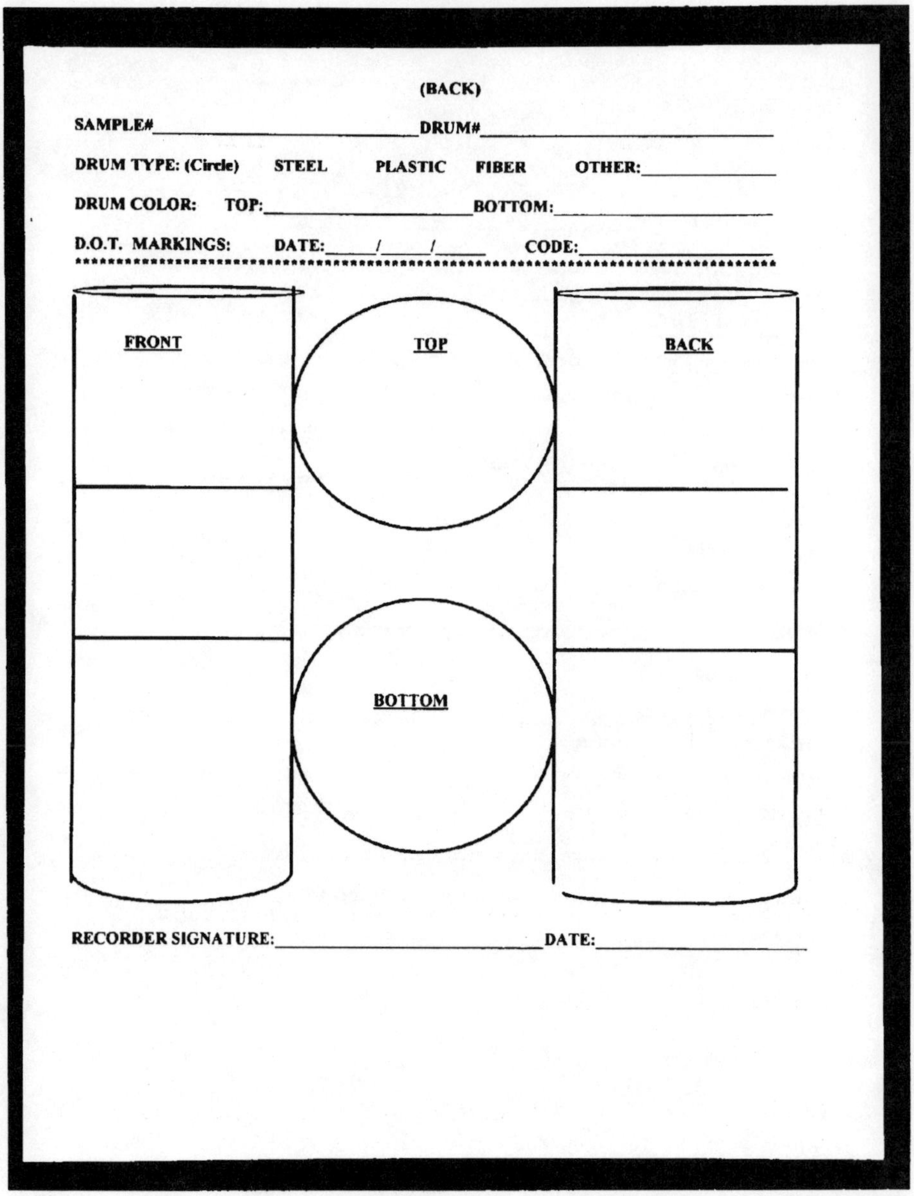

(BACK)

SAMPLE#_____ DRUM#_____

DRUM TYPE: (Circle)   STEEL   PLASTIC   FIBER   OTHER:_____

DRUM COLOR: TOP:_____ BOTTOM:_____

D.O.T. MARKINGS: DATE:_____/_____/_____   CODE:_____

FRONT   TOP   BACK

BOTTOM

RECORDER SIGNATURE:_____/_____/_____ DATE:_____

Figure 30. The rear of the Sample Point Form may be used for the recording
of sample container information.

Chemical Evidence Sampling

Chemical sampling for criminal evidence differs from a regulatory
sampling event in two unique ways. First, the measure of proof in any

criminal environmental prosecution is that of *beyond a reasonable doubt.* This measure of proof leaves very little room for error in the area of evidence collection (see Figure 31). However, regulatory cases require a much lower standard of proof. That standard of proof may be described as *the preponderance of evidence,* which is a much lower level of proof than the standard for a criminal case. The second major difference between the two systems is the need for trace chemical analysis. It is these unique chemical identifiers that may link the suspect to the crime being investigated.

Figure 31. This volatile organic compound sample is not filled to the top as required by SW 846. This type of evidence-collection error may have a serious impact on the prosecution's case.

Sampling hazardous waste so that it may be classified for disposal purposes may be a requirement within the regulatory system; however, it may be of limited value to a criminal investigation. A hazardous waste classified as *flammable* through the use of a flash-point test (see "Chemical Analysis of Criminal Evidence" in Chapter 6) will not supply the environmental investigator with the identity of the chemical constituents which make up the flammable waste. In addition, it is important to select the right analytical test to be performed on the evidence. For instance, if lead (Pb) is a unique chemical identifier for a criminal investigation, it would be important to request that a *total metals* analysis be performed on the sample rather then a *Total Characteristic Leaching Procedure* (TCLP) for metals. The TCLP is a test that the regulatory system uses to determine whether a metal, such as lead, will leach out of a solid waste that is exposed to rain water after it is sent to a landfill for disposal. This test does not subject the sample to the strong oxidizing acid digestion solution that is used for the total metals analysis. In the case of the TCLP analysis, the result for lead (Pb) may be reported as a "*less than*" value, while the results of a total metals analysis, on the same sample, would produce a positive, quantifiable finding for lead (Pb).

In addition to the selection of the correct analysis of the chemical evidence, there are several important principles and investigative techniques which should be utilized when sampling for chemical evidence. These principles and techniques will assist in the furtherance of the criminal investigation and, at the same time, help insure the integrity of the chemical evidence.

Trip Blanks

A trip blank is a sample bottle, normally filled with distilled water, which accompanies the sample collection bottles *before, during, and after* any chemical evidence collection takes place. These trip blanks are then analyzed to insure that no outside contamination or cross contamination has occurred at *any time* during the collection, transportation, and/or storage of the chemical evidence. In addition, a trip blank should be kept with all sampling devices during transportation to the field. This will assist in negating any future claims that sampling device contamination occurred prior to the sampling operation.

Field Blanks

A Field Blank is a sample collected from the sampling device's final rinse prior to reuse. Distilled water is normally used. Shovels, spoons, weighted samplers, dippers, and augers may be used several times during the course of an environmental crime scene. To insure that no outside contamination or cross-contamination (from previous samples) has occurred, a field blank must be utilized in-between samples. If field blanks are *not utilized*, each sample analytical result, after the first sample, may be questioned. Each field blank procedure which occurs during the course of the sampling should be completely documented. This should include information as to the next sample number to be taken, the source and type of water used (distilled), the person's name conducting the rinse, and a description of the sampling device being decontaminated. It is also essential to document that all rinse water used to decontaminate sampling devices has been collected and disposed of properly.

Glove Changes

It is vital that the lead sampler and assistant sampler change their outer gloves in-between each sample, *regardless of whether any apparent glove contamination has occurred*. This procedure insures that no cross-contamination will occur between samples (see Figure 32).

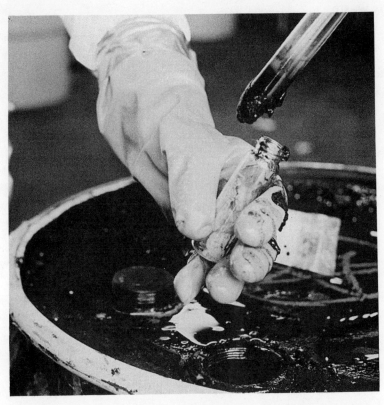

Figure 32. Failure to make a proper change of gloves in this situation, will cause a cross-contamination of the evidence at the next sample point.

Representative Samples

Representative samples are samples exhibiting average properties of the whole waste.[42] When sampling for criminal evidence the environmental investigator must insure that a representative or stratified sample of the whole waste is obtained. Each chemical constituent will have its own specific gravity. When dealing with liquid samples that have more than one chemical present, and are immiscible (do not mix), several separate chemical layers will often form. This effect may be found in many hazardous waste containment vessels. A 55-gallon drum of hazardous waste may contain several layers of different chemical constituents (see Figure 33). A good stratified sample can be taken from a 55-gallon drum through the proper use of a coliwasa tube (see Figure 34). Stratified samples can be obtained from deep tanks and leaching pools by utilizing a weighted sampler at different depths. The environmental investigator must be aware of the fact that any single chemical constituent found, at any layer of the stratum, may become a future forensic chemical link in establishing the origin of the hazardous waste.

TOLUENE:	SPECIFIC GRAVITY .87>
WATER:	SPECIFIC GRAVITY 1.0>
TETRACHLOROETHYLENE:	SPECIFIC GRAVITY 1.62>

Figure 33. Chemical stratification is common in hazardous waste drums.
Proper sampling methods must be utilized to obtain a representative sample of
the hazardous waste.

Figure 34. The white plastic stopper inside this Coliwasa tube is seen here in the closed position. To obtain a proper stratified sample, it must be in the open position when placed into the drum.

Sampling for Trace Analysis

It is rare for the environmental investigator to enter a facility with a search warrant and find an active dischàrge of hazardous waste taking place. It most instances, the environmental investigator will find evidence that a hazardous waste discharge has occurred at some point in the past. To prove that a discharge has taken place in the past, he or she may have to rely on trace chemical analysis to chemically reconstruct the various means and conduits used during the course of the discharge. In investigations involving the abandonment of hazardous waste, it is these trace chemicals which may ultimately link the crime to a particular suspect.

Pipes, Pumps and Hoses

Pipes, pumps and hoses that are suspected of having been used to discharge hazardous waste should be carefully examined for any solid or liquid material that may remain in the interior. If there is no apparent material available to sample, the pipe, pump, and/or hose should be seized. If the item is of such a size as to make it impractical for seizure, the item should be cut. The seized evidence should then be bagged and marked as evidence. Once the evidence is in the laboratory, distilled water should be run through the pipe, pump, and/or hose and collected as evidence. This distilled water rinse should then be analyzed for trace chemicals.

Elbows and Traps

If a sink or other form of washing area is suspected of being a discharge point, it should be examined for an elbow or trap. The elbow or trap should be carefully removed. Any remaining liquid or solid material should be seized as a trace chemical sample. If there is no material available to sample, then the elbow or trap should be bagged and marked for evidence. It should be treated and analyzed in the manner described above for pipes, pumps and hoses.

Vent Pipes, Chimneys, and Stacks

There are two separate sampling methods that should be utilized when examining vent pipes, chimneys, stacks, and other possible air release points for trace chemical evidence (see Figure 35). First, the air inside the discharge conduit should be sampled. Some of the hazardous chemical constituents may be trapped or suspended in the air located inside the conduit. This can be accomplished by utilizing a portable air sampler pump and adsorbent tube. These tubes are packed with various types of adsorbing materials that are capable of capturing contaminants as the sampled air is pulled though the tube. The tube is then marked as evidence and later analyzed using gas chromatography/mass spectroscopy.

The adsorbent tube should be placed into the pipe, chimney, or stack and a known volume of air is then drawn through the tube. When this method is utilized, an ambient air sample (background) should be taken for comparison purposes.

The second sampling method to be utilized is a scrapping of the interior walls of the conduit. These scrapings, which often act as adsorbents, may, when analyzed, identify the actual chemicals that have passed through pipe, chimney, or stack. It is also suggested that the area surrounding the exterior of the conduit be examined. This area may consist of a roof or a wall. If a chemical residue or discoloration is present, this area should be scraped, sampled, and analyzed for trace chemical evidence.

Figure 35. This illegal air pollution source should have its interior sampled for evidence. Note the white chemical residue stains on the roof.

Raw Product

When executing a search warrant at a facility suspected of illegally discharging its hazardous waste, the sampling and subsequent analysis of raw chemical products may prove to be a vital link in the criminal investigation. If chemical compounds are found in the hazardous waste, it is essential that the same chemical compounds also be identified in the raw chemical product. Simply noting labels and/or MSDSs which indicate the presence of these raw chemicals may be insufficient in a criminal prosecution. By sampling and analyzing the raw chemical products and comparing them to other trace chemical analysis completed at the crime scene, the environmental investigator may be able to establish a forensic chemical link between the discharged hazardous waste and the raw chemical product being utilized at the suspect facility.

Volume Reading Techniques

When attempting to enforce certain criminal environmental statutes, it may be necessary to ascertain how much hazardous waste is present at the crime scene. Therefore, proper gallonage measurements must be made and recorded. It is simply inadequate, in a criminal case, to look into a 55-gallon drum and note that it is approximately "half full." Each hazardous waste containment vessel must have its interior and/or exterior measurements taken and recorded. All liquid, solids, and sludges within these containers must have their depths measured and recorded. This information should be placed on a preprinted form for each sample point where the volume of the waste may become a future legal issue (see Figure 29). The names of individuals making these measurements and recordings should also be placed on the forms. In all cases, the measurements should be made after the sampling operations have been completed. This will avoid any future issue regarding outside contamination or cross contamination of the sample points due to volume-measurement procedures.

Each type of hazardous waste container may require a different measurement method. The following suggested methods of measurement may be applied to cans, drums, above ground tanks, below ground tanks, leaching pools, and tankers.

Drums and Cans

To determine the volume of hazardous waste in a drum or can (cylinder), the height of the liquid and the internal radius of the container must be obtained. To measure the height of liquid, a disposable wooden measuring stick should be inserted into the container until it reaches the bottom. The following mathematical formula can be used to determine the volume of hazardous waste present in various sized cylinders: *Volume = (π x (radius)^2 x (height)*. This formula, depending upon the size of the cylinder, will provide a volume in cubic feet or cubic inches. To convert this information into gallons, the following mathematical conversions can be used: *0.13368 ft.^{3} = 1 gallon or 231 in.^{3} = 1 gallon.* When attempting to determine a 55-gallon drum measurement, the height of liquid may also be compared to a standard 55-gallon drum chart (see Table 2). This chart converts known inches of liquid, in a 55-gallon drum, into gallons.

When the wooden measuring stick is withdrawn from the hazardous waste container, a colored pin should be inserted into the stick at the liquid level mark. The measuring stick should then be placed next to the hazardous waste container. The hazardous waste container, sample placard, and measuring stick should then be photographed together (see Figure 36).

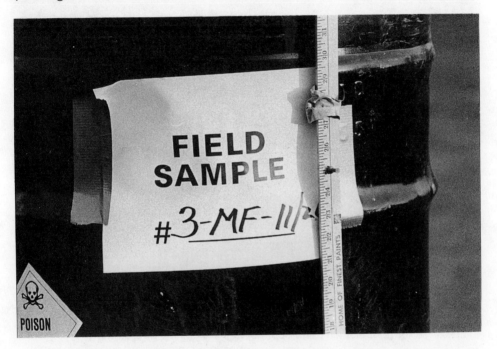

Figure 36. A proper gallonage reading from a 55-gallon hazardous waste drum. Note that the sample number, inches of fluid and the "poison" label, are all visible in one photograph.

Leaching Pools

To obtain the volume of material in a leaching pool the height of liquid and the internal radius of the leaching pool must be determined. A weight, attached to a line, should be slowly lowered into the pool until it reaches the bottom. The line should then be removed from the leaching pool and the liquid height determined by measuring the distance between the weight and the liquid level mark on the line (see Figure 37). This will give the environmental investigator an accurate measurement of the liquid's height. The internal radius of the pool can be measured by inserting an "L"-shaped measuring device into the pool. The radius measurement, combined with the liquid's height, will supply the environmental investigator with the necessary information to complete the mathematical formula for a cylinder volume as described above.

Figure 37. After sampling has been completed, the suspected leaching pool is measured for pool diameter and depth of liquid. Note the sample team's safety lines and communication equipment.

Above-Ground Tanks

When recording measurements for above-ground tanks, the liquid's height in the tank and the internal radius of the tank must obtained. The liquid height measurement can be obtained by using the weighted line method described above for measuring leaching pools. The internal radius may be obtained by determining the tank's external radius and subtracting the thickness of the tank walls. The internal radius measurement, combined with the liquid's height, will supply the environmental investigator with the necessary information to complete the mathematical formula for a cylinder's volume as described above.

Below-Ground Tanks

Below-ground tanks may offer some difficulties in obtaining exact measurements. It may become necessary to rely on building plans and tank registry documents to obtain exact dimensions. However, excavations and soil borings can be made in an effort to locate the perimeter of the tank. Once the overall size of the tank is determined, the height of the liquid and the tank's internal radius can be obtained by using the method described above. To determine the underground tank's volume, the mathematical formula for cylinder volumes should be used.

Hazardous Waste Tankers

When attempting to determine the gallonage reading of a tanker, the environmental investigator should first inspect the tanker for baffles. The tanker may be divided into several separate compartments (see Figure 38). Each compartment may require a separate stratified chemical sample and volume measurement. This volume measurement should include the distance from baffle-to-baffle as well as the total length and depth of the tank itself. The depth of tank and the height of liquid can be obtained by utilizing the weighted line method described above. The tanker should also be inspected for some type of metering device. This device may offer some information as to how much liquid material is in the tanker. Also, the name of the tanker's manufacturer should be noted. The manufacturer can be contacted and a tank chart obtained. The tank chart may convert liquid levels (feet and inches) into a gallonage reading. The manufacturer may also offer information regarding the tanker's baffled compartments.

Figure 38. This tanker was illegally transporting hazardous waste. A stratified chemical sample and volume reading was taken from each compartment.

Photographing the Chemical Evidence

The environmental investigator may wish to photograph the chemical evidence next to or on top of the sample point (i.e., on top of a 55-gallon drum). If this type of photography is to be done, extreme caution must be exercised. Sample points, by nature, normally have some form of contamination surrounding them. This could be the floor area under a slop sink or the top of a hazardous waste drum. Some of the chemical constituents found in the surrounding contaminated area *may not* be present in the hazardous waste which has just been sampled. If the chemical evidence is to be photographed at the sample point, a protective layer should be placed between the contaminated surface and the chemical evidence. This may be a plastic sheet or a tray used to carry clean sample containers. Under no circumstances should the sample containers come into contact with the contaminated sample point surfaces.

Labeling the Chemical Evidence

Properly filled out sample-container labels will help prevent any future misidentification of the chemical evidence. Sample labels should be placed onto the sample containers prior to taking the sample. "The label should indicate the sample number, name of the collector, place of collection, and the date and time collected. Gummed labels or tags may be used."[43]

Sealing the Chemical Evidence

Sample seals are used to detect unauthorized tampering of the chemical evidence. The seals should contain the same information as listed on the sample label. The seal must be affixed to the containers before the samples leave the custody of the Sample team. "It must be affixed in such a way that it is necessary to break it in order to open the sample container."[44]

Another acceptable method is to place the sample containers and the trip blanks, into see-through plastic evidence bags. The evidence bags are then heat-sealed closed. This method has several advantages. The sealed evidence envelope adds another layer of protection against possible outside contamination. In addition, the sample label information can be clearly seen through the envelope. Also, a simple inspection of the evidence envelope will determine if any unauthorized tampering has taken place.

The Log Book

"All information relating to the collection of chemical evidence must be recorded in a bound logbook."[45] Entries in this log book should include the following information:

- Location of the sampling point.
- Name and address of field contact (if applicable).
- Waste generator and address (if known).
- Type of process producing the waste (if known).
- The waste matrix (sludge, liquid, solid).
- Suspected waste composition and concentrations (if known).
- Sample number and volume of sample taken.
- Purpose of sampling.
- Description of sample point and sampling methodology.
- Date and time of collection.
- Collector's sample identification number(s) (Field Sample #).

• Sample distribution and how transported.
• References, such as maps or photographs of the sampling site.
• Field observations.
• Any field tests or measurements made.
• Signature of personnel responsible for observations.

Each environmental crime scene will have its own unique characteristics. Therefore, the types of entries made in the log may vary. However, if the log entries can clearly reestablish the chemical evidence collection events, without relying on the memories of the sample team, then those entries made should be considered sufficient.

It should be noted that the logbook and the preprinted sample sheet forms described earlier have two different functions. While the logbook requirements are used to reestablish the chemical evidence collection events, the preprinted sample sheets and their data supply the environmental investigator with the information needed to further the investigation.

Chain-of-Custody

In order to maintain the integrity of the chemical evidence, a proper chain-of-custody must exist. The chain-of-custody should be traceable through documentation. The documentation should indicate who had custody of the chemical evidence from the time it was collected all the way through the analytical process. The signature of each individual taking custody of the evidence should appear on the documentation. The environmental investigator's responsibility for evidence integrity does not end with the shipping of the chemical evidence to a laboratory. The laboratory should be contacted and their chain-of-custody procedures reviewed prior to the shipment of any chemical evidence.

Chemical Analysis Request Sheet

The chemical analysis request sheet is a document which is partially completed by the lead sampler at the crime scene. Information obtained from the logbook may be used to complete this document. The document accompanies the samples to the laboratory, where the remainder of the information is filled in by laboratory personnel. It is this document that alerts the laboratory as to the type or types of analysis that are to be completed. As stated earlier, one of the most difficult decisions facing the environmental investigator is choosing the proper analysis for the chemical evidence seized. It is vital that the necessary type(s) of analysis be determined prior to the completion and submission of this document.

Transporting Chemical Evidence

At the closing of the environmental crime scene, the chemical evidence must be prepared for transportation. The chemical evidence should be placed in a cooler in such a way as to prevent accidental breakage. The evidence should be accompanied by the trip blanks, any field blanks, chain-of-custody sheets, and requests for analysis sheets. Most chemical evidence is best preserved by refrigerating it at 4°C; however, SW 846 (or a particular state's equivalent requirements) should be consulted directly regarding holding times and preservation requirements for individual chemical compounds. The cooler itself should be secured in such a way as to prevent it from being damaged during transportation. "The chemical evidence should be delivered to the laboratory for analysis as soon as practicable. This should usually be done within 1 or 2 days after sampling."[46]

The environmental investigator should inspect and inventory the chemical evidence prior to the evidence leaving the crime scene. It is the information from this inventory that should be utilized if a receipt is to be left at the environmental crime scene (see "The Warrant Execution" in Chapter 2).

Packaging and Shipping Chemical Evidence

There are two main areas of concern when shipping chemical evidence to a laboratory for analysis. The first is the proper packaging of the chemical evidence. The packaging must meet all Federal Department of Transportation regulations and all International Air Transport Association requirements. Federal regulations "classify those materials which the Department of Transportation has designated as hazardous materials for the purposes of transportation and prescribe the requirements for the shipping papers, package markings, labeling, and transport vehicle placarding applicable to the shipment and transportation of those hazardous materials."[47] Many different factors will determine the packaging requirements for the chemical evidence. These factors may include the volume of the material, the chemical characteristics of the material, the type of chemical (if known), and the type of transportation to be utilized (i.e., air cargo, air passenger, ground vehicles). The Federal Department of Transportation regulations as well as the International Air Transport Association requirements should be consulted directly when attempting to determine the proper packaging requirements for shipping chemical evidence.

The second area of concern is the maintaining of the integrity of the chemical evidence during shipment. It is essential that the environmental investigator be able to prove that no outside chemical contamination occurred during the transportation process. This is accomplished by insuring that the trip blanks accompany the chemical evidence at all times. In addition, the chemical evidence should be sealed in such a way (i.e., sealing tape or heat sealed bags) so that the receiving laboratory will be able to determine if any unauthorized tampering has taken place during the shipping process.

Chapter 6

CHEMICAL ANALYSIS OF
CRIMINAL EVIDENCE

Choosing the Laboratory

The scientific evidence in a criminal environmental prosecution may be subjected to challenge during the trial phase of the case. As a result of this, choosing of the proper laboratory for chemical evidence analysis becomes a vital issue. There is a long list of criteria that must be established before the environmental investigator can begin transporting or shipping chemical evidence to a laboratory. The environmental investigator must first determine if a laboratory certification program exists within his or her jurisdiction. These programs are normally administered by state agencies which, through the use of proficiency tests and inspections, certify individual laboratories to conduct various environmental analyses. A listing of these certified laboratories can usually be obtained by contacting the governing state agency. Once the list has been obtained, or if a preexisting contract exists with a certified laboratory, the environmental investigator should contact and, if possible, visit the laboratory. During this contact, the environmental investigator should insure that the laboratory is capable of handling criminal evidence in an acceptable manner and is capable of providing the analysis needed to further the investigation.

Method Choice

There are many different approved methods for analyzing chemical evidence.[48] A *specific* chemical compound or element may be analyzed using several different methods of analysis. To prove that a chemical sample is a hazardous waste may require analyses to determine its characteristics, such as flash point or pH. It may also be necessary to analyze a chemical sample in order to determine if a specific chemical compound, sometimes at trace (low) levels, exists in the sample. It is with this specific and trace chemical analysis that the environmental investigator must be certain that the appropriate method of analysis is utilized. A laboratory conducting an analysis for volatile organic compounds (VOCs) may utilize the approved gas chromatographic Method #8021B for a specific organic compound. However, this method may not positively identify *all* of the organic compounds present in the sample due to the lack of mass spectrometry confirmation. For example, using this method, carbon tetrachloride and 1,2-dichloroethane are retained by the column in the gas chromatograph and appear as one peak (see Figure 39). This type of analysis may be devastating to the criminal prosecution when attempting to build a criminal case based upon a forensic chemical connection. When dealing with trace volatile organic compound analysis, one the best methods to use is Method # 8260B, which utilizes gas chromatography/mass spectrometry (see Figure 40). The instrumentation in this method makes it possible to positively identify a compound by its mass spectrum. The mass spectrum of an organic compound is equivalent to identifying a person by their fingerprint.

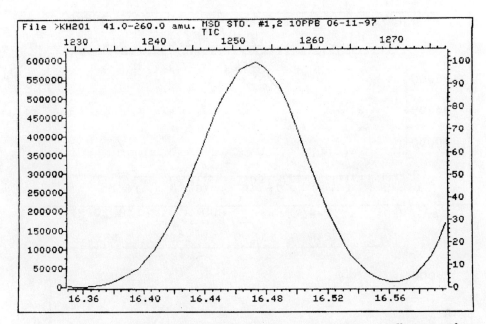

Figure 39. Method #8021B. What appears to be a single peak is actually two peaks, carbon tetrachloride and 1,2 dichloroethane. The detector responds to both compounds and, because the gas chromatograph could not separate them, it is not certain if one or both are producing the peak. Therefore, neither can be positively identified or quantified.

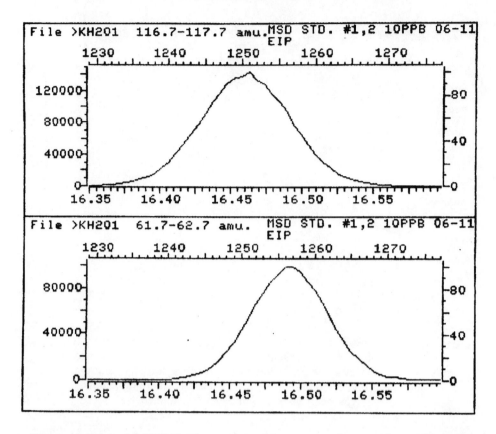

Figure 40. Method #8260 B. The mass spectrometer can detect and quantify both carbon tetrachloride and the 1,2 dichloroethane even though they co-elute.

Method Certification

The chemical evidence to be examined by the laboratory may require several different analytical methods. Analysis for characteristics as well as trace chemical analysis may be needed. The environmental investigator must insure that the laboratory is currently certified for the approved method, for each individual analyte (chemical compound or element) and sample matrix (air, water, soil, etc.), to be used to analyze the chemical evidence being submitted. An expired, suspended or revoked certification may have a devastating effect on the prosecution's case during a criminal trial.

Holding Time Requirements

Each individual analytical method will indicate the maximum allowable holding time for a sample. This period of time begins at the collection of the chemical evidence. The sample *must* be analyzed within this allowable holding time. The holding times vary based upon the sample type and method of analysis and may range from several hours (fecal coliform) to several months (certain metals). The environmental investigator must insure that the laboratory can meet these holding time requirements prior to the transportation or shipment of any chemical evidence.

Laboratory Chain-of-Custody Protocols

The laboratory's chain-of-custody protocols should be reviewed by the environmental investigator prior to the transportation or shipment of any chemical evidence. Information regarding evidence access and storage should be fully documented by the laboratory. This should include detailed information regarding which individual(s) handled the chemical evidence during the analysis phase and information as to which individuals had access to the chemical evidence during storage.

Every effort should be made to limit the number of individuals involved in the analytical process. It may be the practice of the laboratory to have one individual do the digestion on a particular sample, another may calibrate the analytical instrument, another may load the sample onto the instrument while a different individual may read the data and complete the laboratory report. Each one of these individuals may be subject to direct testimony and cross-examination during a criminal trial. This type of scientific evidence handling may place an unneeded burden upon the prosecutor. By discussing these issues with the laboratory director prior to the transportation or shipment of the chemical evidence, the environmental investigator may be able to limit the number of individuals who may be called to testify at a later date.

Laboratory Personnel Credentials

When identifying the laboratory personnel who will be conducting the analysis, it is important that their personal credentials be established. It is essential that these individuals meet the training and education requirements in their respective areas of expertise. It is quite possible that, at some future date, these individuals may become key prosecution witnesses. Their training and education may become an issue if the scientific evidence is challenged at trial. The environmental investigator should make every effort to avoid allowing inexperienced laboratory personnel to conduct analysis on the chemical evidence. The best witnesses will be those who are highly trained, well educated, and have prior experience in testifying at criminal trials. This can be accomplished by examining the credentials of laboratory personnel and discussing any concerns in this area with the laboratory director prior to the transportation or shipment of the chemical evidence.

Laboratory Postanalysis

A laboratory's postanalysis activities may become critical to the prosecution's criminal case. The saving of all notes and computer records may be a legal requirement in some jurisdictions. The environmental investigator, by meeting with the prosecutor, can determine what, if any, legal requirements exist in this area. Should there be a requirement that all notes and computer records be maintained by the laboratory, the environmental investigator must relay this information to the laboratory director. In addition, the environmental investigator should determine what procedures the laboratory utilizes for the storage of the chemical evidence after analysis. The remaining chemical evidence must be stored and maintained properly until such time that the prosecutor indicates, in writing, that the evidence may be disposed of or released.

Chemical Analysis: Instrumentation and Methodologies

There are many instruments and analytical methodologies that may be used for the analysis of chemical evidence. The different types of instruments used are too numerous to include here and, as stated earlier, chemical evidence may be analyzed using many different, yet acceptable, analytical methods. However, the majority of analysis completed for criminal environmental cases utilize four particular instruments and a limited number of methods. A full description of these analytical methods may be found in SW 846. The descriptions that follow are designed to give the environmental investigator a basic understanding a particular instrument's capabilities and applications. The analytical methods listed with the instruments are some of the more common ones used in the investigation of cases involving suspected hazardous wastes.

Gas Chromatography/Mass Spectrometry

A gas chromatograph/mass spectrometer (GC/MS) is an instrument used to detect the presence and concentration of numerous volatile and semivolatile organic chemical compounds in a sample (see Figure 41). Although the use of the GC/MS is common to the analysis of both volatile and semivolatile compounds, it is the preparation of the sample that decides which group is actually being determined. This instrument has the capability to positively identify and measure the concentration of organic chemical compounds in the parts-per-billion (ppb)range. It is an essential tool in determining the presence of various chemical compounds which may constitute a hazardous waste or a hazardous substance.

In the volatile and semivolatile analysis, the GC/MS must be calibrated using standards of known purity and concentrations. These standards are analyzed in the same manner as the chemical evidence. Once analyzed, the results for the calibration standards are reviewed by the analyst to verify that the GC/MS correctly identified all of the compound in the standard and produced an accurate result for each. Once this has been accomplished, a measured amount of a sample is injected into the instrument to determine if any organic compound(s) of interest are present, and if so, at what concentration(s). In a volatile organic compound analysis, this would be accomplished by placing a measured portion of the sample (liquid or solid) into a glass impinger. The impinger is part of a sample concentrating device that purges (strips) the VOCs from the sample matrix via a stream of helium gas. For the VOC analysis of a solid sample, the impinger must be heated to 40°C. The helium gas stream is then passed through a trap containing adsorbents that recapture the VOCs. The trap is then heated and the flow of the helium is reversed through the trap. This causes the release of the VOCs. They are then transferred and cryogenically trapped using liquid nitrogen (-150°C) at the head of the capillary column. The cryogenic trap is then rapidly heated to 200°C, causing the frozen VOCs to liquefy, vaporize, and pass into the capillary column. The capillary column is located in the oven chamber of the gas chromatograph and is purged with a constant flow of helium gas. The time at which this transfer takes place is called the "injection time." The capillary column is normally constructed of fused silica and its interior surface has the capability to separate organic compounds from the sample as they pass through. At the "injection time," the gas chromatograph is programmed to increase the temperature of the oven in order to facilitate the separation of the organic compounds. In general, compounds with lower boiling points pass through and exit (elute) the column first. The end of the capillary column is interfaced with a detector (mass spectrometer). The "retention time" of a compound is the time it takes from the "injection time" until the compound reaches the mass spectrometer. As the chemical compounds exit the column, they enter the ion source of the mass spectrometer. Here they are exposed to an electron beam, which imparts enough energy into the molecule of the organic compound to rupture some of the chemical bonds holding the molecule together. This process of fragmentation is called "electron ionization." Electron ionization produces positively-, negatively-, or neutrally-charged fragments. In this method, the positively-charged fragments are accelerated into a mass filter. The mass filter then separates the fragments based upon their mass. It is these fragments and retention times that are measured by the mass spectrometer. The fragment ions are then compared to the fragment ions of the previously run standards. It is this comparison that supplies the final identification and quantification of the organic compound(s) present in the sample.

If the result for a particular compound exceeds the linear range of the calibration curve, the sample must be diluted and reanalyzed. This is accomplished by diluting a measured amount of the sample with "organic free" distilled water or high purity methanol. Once diluted, a measured volume of the diluted sample is reanalyzed. The result of this analysis is corrected for the initial sample dilution to calculate the actual concentrations in the sample.

The following Analytical Methods utilize the GC/MS for the identification and quantification of volatile and semivolatile compounds.

This includes those chemical compounds identified as hazardous wastes based upon their *toxicity*.[49]

1. Method 8260B: Volatile Organic Compounds by Gas Chromatography/Mass Spectrometry–Capillary Column Technique.

2. Method 8270C: Semi-volatile Organic Compounds by Gas Chromatography/Mass Spectrometry–Capillary Column Technique.

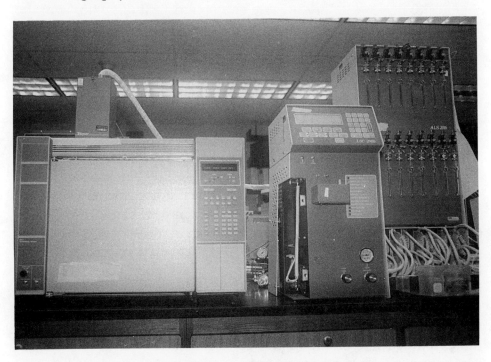

Figure 41. A gas chromatograph/mass spectrometer (GC/MS) used to detect and quantify volatile and semivolatile chemical compounds. Note the glass impingers on the right side of the photograph.

Inductively Coupled Plasma/Atomic Emissions Spectrometer

The inductively coupled plasma/atomic emissions spectrometer (ICP/AES) is used to perform elemental analyses (see Figure 42). One of its primary functions is to analyze for toxic metals such as cadmium (Cd) and lead (Pb). This instrument is also known as the inductively coupled plasma/*optical* emission spectrometer (ICP/OES).

The ICP/AES is capable of detecting and quantitatively measuring metals in the parts-per-billion (ppb) range. This instrument will identify and quantify hazardous wastes and substances by their toxic metal content.

A digestion procedure must be completed on the sample before it can be analyzed on the ICP/AES. This procedure requires the introduction of an oxidizing acid solution into the sample. The sample is then heated to insure that the toxic metals are in solution and not chemically bonded to any organic compound. If the sample is in the form of a petroleum product, xylene may be added to the sample to reduce its viscosity. However, if xylene is used to prepare the sample, the calibration standards must also be prepared in xylene.

Prior to introducing a sample into the ICP/AES, the instrument must be electronically and thermally stabilized. During this stabilization period, a solution containing distilled water and nitric acid is pumped into an aspirator (nebulizer). Once this has been completed, the instrument must be calibrated using quantitative calibration standards. These standards are solutions containing known and exact amounts of metals. The metals contained in the standard are the same metals which will be searched for in the sample. The standards are then analyzed in the same manner as the samples and the results reported. These results are reviewed by an analyst to verify that the ICP/AES is correctly identifying and quantifying the metals within an acceptable range.

In the actual analysis, the sample is placed into a glass beaker. It is then pumped through a Teflon tube into the nebulizer. The sample is then aspirated into an argon plasma. The argon plasma, which looks like a flame, reaches a temperature range of 8000°C to 12,000°C (see Figure 43). The plasma excites the atoms of the elements (metals), causing the electrons of the element to jump into an excited state. The electrons then fall back to a less energetic state and in doing so, cause a photon (light) to be released. The wavelength of the emitted light will be the means by which the metal in the sample is identified. The intensity of the light emitted is directly proportional to the amount (concentration) of a metal present in the sample. The concentration of the metal in the sample is determined by the comparison of the light intensity emitted during the analysis of the sample to that of the calibration standards.

The following Analytical Methods utilize the ICP/AES for the identification and quantification of metals in solution. This includes those metals identified as hazardous wastes based upon their *toxicity*.[50]

1. Method 6010B: Inductively Coupled Plasma/Atomic Emission Spectroscopy.
2. Method 6020: Inductively Coupled Plasma/Mass Spectrometry.
3. Method 1310A: Extraction Procedure (EP) Toxicity Test Method and Structural Integrity Test.
4. Method 1311: Toxicity Characteristic Leaching Procedure (TCLP).

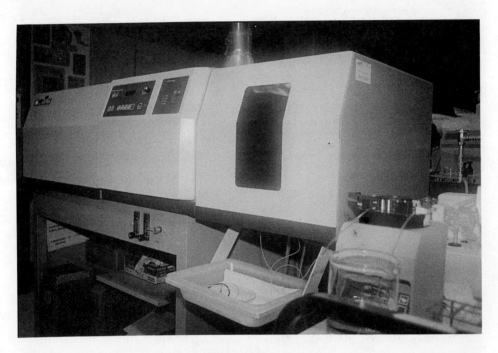

Figure 42. An inductively coupled plasma/atomic emissions spectrometer (ICP/AES) used to perform elemental analyses. The argon plasma chamber is located behind the darkened rectangular glass panel.

Figure 43. This chamber, inside the ICP/AES, contains the argon plasma. The argon plasma reaches a temperature range of 8,000°C to 12,000°C.

pH Meter

In criminal environmental investigations the electronic pH meter is used to determine the pH of chemical evidence (see Figure 44). The hydrogen ion (H+) concentration in a sample determines whether it is acidic (low pH) or alkaline (high pH). A substance that has a pH of 0 is extremely acidic. A substance that has a pH of 14 is extremely alkaline. A pH of 7 is considered neutral.

This instrument consists of a pH electrode, a reference electrode (or a glass electrode combining both) and a meter that measures the millivolt signal from the electrodes. This meter converts and displays the pH value.

The pH meter must be calibrated before use. This is accomplished by placing the electrodes (or combination electrode) into buffer solutions of a known pH. A minimum of two buffer solutions must be used and should bracket (one higher and one lower) the suspected pH value of the sample. The values of the buffers selected must be at least 3 pH units apart. For example, one buffer solution could have a pH value of 7 (neutral) and the second one a pH value of 4.0 (acidic) or 10.0 (alkaline). Once calibration has been completed, the electrodes must be well rinsed with distilled water. The electrodes may then be placed into the sample and a recording of the pH measurement made.

The following Analytical Method utilizes the pH meter to determine the hazardous waste characteristic of *corrosivity*.[51]

Method 9040B: pH Electrometric Measurement.

Figure 44. An electronic pH meter used to determine the hazardous waste characteristic of corrosivity. The sample being tested here has a pH of approximately 7 (neutral).

Pensky-Martens Closed-Cup Tester

The Pensky-Martens closed-cup tester is used to determine the flash point (ignitability) of the chemical evidence (see Figure 45). The chemical evidence may be in the form of a liquid, with or without a surface film, or nonfilterable suspended solids. The flash point is the lowest temperature at which a flame, or other ignition source, ignites the vapor that exists above the surface of a liquid. The sample is placed into the closed cup of the tester and slowly heated at a rate of 5-6°C per minute. As the liquid is heated, the vapor pressure above the surface increases. During this heating, the liquid sample is constantly stirred (90-120 rpm) and is exposed to an ignition source at each degree centigrade. The temperature at which ignition of the vapor above the liquid is detected or observed is the flash point (see Figure 46). The accuracy of the Pensky-Martens closed-cup tester is checked before analyzing any chemical evidence by determining the flash point of a known chemical (i.e., p-xylene = 27°C).

The following Analytical Method utilizes the Pensky-Martens closed-cup tester to determine the hazardous waste characteristic of *ignitability*.[52]

1. Method 1010: Pensky-Martens Closed-Cup Method for Determining Ignitability.

Figure 45. A Pensky-Martens closed cup tester. The closed cup (attached to a wooden handle) is inserted into the apparatus and slowly heated.

Figure 46. The xylene in this test sample was heated to its flash point of 27°C. The flash occured at the moment this temperature was reached.

Chapter 7

HAZARDOUS WASTE STING OPERATIONS

Sting operations have been used by law enforcement for many years. Traditionally, these techniques have been used in cases involving narcotics and stolen property. They may range from a simple narcotics buy-and-bust operation, to a more elaborate undercover fencing operation. The fencing operation may involve a storefront, staffed by undercover police officers. Each criminal transaction which takes place within the store is audio- and video-recorded. One of the main goals in these types of operations is to gather evidence against individuals involved in criminal activity. With this goal in mind, the sting operation can become a valuable tool to the environmental investigator.

As with all sting operations, the environmental investigator must be aware of the entrapment issue. It should not appear, at any time, that the undercover officer is planting the criminal idea into the mind of the suspect. To avoid this type of problem, the environmental investigator should consult with the prosecutor in the planning stage of any sting operation. With the assistance and guidance of the prosecutor, the environmental investigator will be able to develop the legally sufficient language which will be used during the course of recorded conversations with the suspect or suspects.

Hazardous waste sting operations come in a variety of forms. The environmental investigator may wish to focus on illegal hazardous waste transporters or hazardous waste generators suspected of illegally disposing of their wastes. Each type of hazardous waste sting operation will require its own unique approach and a detailed written plan.

Targeting Suspect Hazardous Waste Transporters

One of the main focus points for criminal environmental investigations is the illegal hazardous waste transporter. These individuals will unlawfully remove hazardous waste from various generators and will eventually dispose of it illegally. They may bring the hazardous waste to an illegal storage facility or they may abandon it at some remote location. Their illegal activities may be brought to the attention of law enforcement through information supplied by informants, hazardous waste generators, or complaints made by legitimate hazardous waste transporters. These illegal transporters obtain new business by offering extremely low prices for hazardous waste removal. A typical plating operation may be paying as much as $1,300 for the proper removal of one 55-gallon drum of cyanide sludge. The suspect transporter may offer to remove the same drum at a cost of $50.00. In order to gain the evidence necessary to arrest and eventually convict these individuals, the environmental investigator may wish to use a hazardous waste sting operation that involves the creation of a fictitious hazardous waste generator.

Planning the Operation.

The environmental investigator must address such issues as operation costs, manpower requirements, electronic surveillance needs and the location of the undercover hazardous waste generator. In addition, he or she must decide upon the type of waste which is to be offered for unlawful transport and possible disposal. There are several options available to the environmental investigator in this type of hazardous waste sting operation. The first option involves waste that appears hazardous, but is in fact nonhazardous. This can be accomplished by filling 55-gallon drums with vegetable dyed water. Various nonhazardous ingredients, such as garlic, may be added to the water to produce a pungent odor. One of the key problems associated with this type of operation is the fact that the waste *is* nonhazardous. In many jurisdiction, this type of activity may not be criminal in nature. In other jurisdictions, it may be considered an "attempted" criminal act. The legal ramifications of using nonhazardous waste, in the place of hazardous waste, must be thoroughly discussed with the prosecutor during the planning stage.

The next option available to the environmental investigator is the use of real hazardous waste. This type of operation has several serious aspects which must be carefully considered prior to implementation. Due to the fact that the waste is hazardous, the suspects and innocent civilians may have their health and safety placed in jeopardy. There is the possibility of serious physical injury and/or death should an accident occur during the loading or transportation of the hazardous waste. Unless these concerns can be addressed in such a way as to reduce the risks described above, this type of operation should be avoided.

The third option available to the environmental investigator is to use waste materials that are legally defined as hazardous wastes, but are present in such small quantities and concentrations, that the risk of accidental exposure is minimal. In some jurisdictions, such items as waste oil, lead contaminated soils and/or paint wastes may be considered hazardous wastes. If an accidental release should occur during the loading or illegal transportation of these types of low level hazardous waste, the possibility of physical injury would be negligible. The prosecutor must be consulted prior to the implementation of any plan involving the use of actual hazardous waste.

Whenever actual hazardous waste is to be offered to a suspected transporter for removal, the environmental investigator must insure that the waste has been properly sampled and analyzed. Proper sampling and analysis is needed to prove that the waste was hazardous at the time of removal. The environmental investigator should also discuss with the prosecutor the possible need for obtaining an EPA hazardous waste generator identification number.[53]

Establishing the Undercover Generator

Establishing what appears to be a legitimate generator of hazardous waste requires the use of a building which contains an office and a small, but separate, manufacturing area. There is no need to establish an actual functioning manufacturing area. The perception that one exists is the only requirement. The office should be equipped with the proper audio and video surveillance equipment which will allow for the proper recording of all conversations with any potential suspects. The office should also be equipped with a working telephone, file cabinets, desks and any other items that will give the appearance of a legitimate office area.

All hazardous waste containers which are to be removed by the suspect transporter should be stored outside the building. This area should also be placed under audio and video surveillance. All conversation involving the criminal transactions should be held in the office area or in the outside drum storage area. By limiting the suspects movements to these two areas, the environmental investigator will be insuring the proper recording of any criminal transactions.

Hazardous Waste Containers

The hazardous waste containers must be marked in such a manner as to clearly indicate that they contain hazardous waste. To accomplish this, the drums should be placarded with hazardous waste labels, flammable liquid waste labels, acid labels and/or poison labels. Multiple labels of the same type should be placed on each drum. Each label should clearly show the type of hazard. One of the most effective labels to use is the *Poison* label. The word *Poison* should be accompanied by a picture of a skull and crossbones. This is the international symbol used to identify poisons. These actions will assist the prosecutor in countering any future legal defense regarding the suspect's *knowledge* as to the hazardous nature of the waste material. In addition, each drum must be marked in such a surreptitious manner as to allow for future identification should the illegal transporter remove all of the identifying labels. This can be accomplished by placing a small identifiable tool mark on the lip of the drum. Also, a unique numbering system can be stenciled onto the drum. This information should be added to the last line of the preexisting Department of Transportation information. However, the environmental investigator should expect that any visible markings on the drums may be removed by the suspect.

Hazardous Waste Removal

The removal of the hazardous waste by the suspect transporter should be recorded using still photography and videotape. The suspects should be photographed in such a way as to allow for future positive identification. Surveillance teams should then follow the illegal transporter to any ultimate storage facility or disposal point. A search warrant should be obtained if the hazardous waste containers have been taken to an illegal hazardous waste storage facility. The search-warrant team should exercise extreme caution when entering this type of facility. The storage of incompatible hazardous wastes and the possibility of existing spillage may cause severe hazards for the entry team. If the hazardous waste containers are taken to a remote disposal point and abandoned, every effort should be made to photograph and videotape the illegal transporter's disposal of the containers.

The requirements for a successful hazardous waste sting operation in this area are simple. There must be proper planning, legally sufficient recorded conversations with the suspects, proper labeling and marking of the hazardous waste containers, and proper surveillance.

Targeting Suspect Hazardous Waste Generators

The illegal disposal of hazardous waste by generators is normally accomplished in one of three ways. First, the waste may be illegally disposed of on the generator's property. This is normally accomplished by discharging the waste directly to the ground or into underground leaching pools. Second, the generator may abandon the hazardous waste in an area away from its point of generation. The third option open to the hazardous waste generator is to hire an illegal hazardous waste transporter. A successful sting operation involving the creation of a fictitious illegal hazardous waste transporter, normally requires the use of a good informant. The informant may be someone in the business of hazardous waste transportation and/or hazardous waste disposal. It is this type of individual who can provide the environmental investigator with the identities of those hazardous waste generators who are anxious to participate in this type of illegal activity.

This type of hazardous waste sting operation is extremely complex and requires a great deal of planning. In this type of operation, an undercover environmental investigator will be posing as an illegal hazardous waste transporter. This investigator, along with other members of the operations team, will be receiving, transporting, sampling and eventually, disposing of the hazardous waste.

Planning the Operation

The planning stage of this type of hazardous waste sting operation should address such issues as office rental space, utilities, potential overtime expenditures, truck rental costs, permit requirements, hazardous waste sampling and analysis costs, and hazardous waste disposal costs. Each individual assigned to the investigation should have a written description of his or her duties and responsibilities. In addition, there should be an itemized list of each piece of equipment that is to be utilized during the investigation. This should include surveillance equipment, safety equipment, transportation equipment, and any equipment needed for the sampling of the hazardous waste. In addition, the plan should include a written *standard operating procedure* for the loading, transporting, sampling, storage, and ultimate disposal of the hazardous waste.

A policy should also be established as to what types of hazardous wastes will be accepted for transport. For safety reasons, hazardous wastes which are extremely toxic, reactive with air, or shock sensitive should be avoided at all times. A proper investigation into the manufacturing process of a suspect generator will, in all likelihood, reveal the types of raw chemical products utilized at the facility and the types of hazardous waste generated. This should be completed prior to the removal of any hazardous waste by the undercover environmental investigators. In addition to the types of wastes to be accepted, a standard should be set for the types of hazardous waste containers that will be accepted for transport. Large tanks and leaking drums may cause serious loading and transportation difficulties for the undercover environmental investigators handling the hazardous waste. It is suggested that only those hazardous wastes contained in well-conditioned drums be accepted for transport.

The transportation and ultimate proper disposal of the hazardous waste may require a transporter's EPA identification number and/or a special permit to transport the hazardous waste.[54] These issues should be discussed with the prosecutor during the planning stage of the sting operation.

Personnel Requirements

Personnel assigned to this type of sting operation should be broken into teams. The informant should work with an undercover investigator. These two individuals, acting as a team, will be responsible for all contacts made with the suspect generators. Once the informant has made an introduction to the suspect generator, the undercover investigator should then become the lead contact person in any future dealings or communications. This will help insure that any future conversations with the suspect will meet those legal requirements set forth by the prosecutor. If allowable under local law, all telephone conversations and personal meetings between the suspect generators and the undercover environmental investigator should be recorded.

A surveillance team should be created. This team should be responsible for all photography and videotaping of transactions and discussions, including any transactions which take place at the undercover investigator's office, the generator's facility, or any other location where part or all of the criminal transaction takes place. These surveillance recordings should include the filming of any exchange of money as well as any loading and removal of the hazardous waste containers.

A hazardous waste transportation team should be created. This team will be comprised of those individuals who will have the responsibility for loading and transporting the hazardous waste. It is essential that these individuals be properly trained and certified in the handling of hazardous materials.

Once the hazardous waste has been transported to a predetermined location, a chemical evidence team will be responsible for the gathering of all chemical and physical evidence that is associated with the hazardous waste containers. This team should be properly trained and certified in the areas of hazardous waste sampling and the collection of physical evidence.

The Vehicle

The proper vehicle and vehicle equipment must be chosen for the safe transportation of the hazardous waste drums. Consideration must be given to maximum load capacity and weight distribution. The loading of ten 55-gallon drums will require at least 35 square feet of cargo space. These same ten drums may have a total weight exceeding 6,000 pounds. The vehicle must be equipped with a lift gate so that each drum may be safely loaded onto it. A load stabilization bar should be utilized during transportation to insure that no shifting of the load occurs. A drum dolly should be present onboard the vehicle. This device will assist in the moving of the drums once they are in the vehicle. In addition, the cab of the vehicle should contain safety, communication, and fire-fighting equipment.

Establishing the Undercover Office

Establishing a functional undercover office may become necessary prior to the commencement of the sting operation. If an undercover office is utilized, it should be equipped with both audio and video recording capabilities. Some hazardous waste generators may insist upon meeting the undercover investigator and/or the informant at a location other than the suspect facility. If this situation should arise, the undercover office can be used. The controlled environment of an undercover office will normally produce the highest quality recordings.

The Criminal Transaction

Normally, the exchange of money will take place at the time the hazardous waste containers are actually removed. The exchange of money should be recorded by the undercover investigator and, if possible, by the surveillance team. If possible, the transaction should take place near the hazardous waste loading operation. This may enable the surveillance team to videotape the exchange and loading operation at the same time.

The hazardous waste transportation team should exercise caution when loading the hazardous waste containers onto the vehicle. All safety protocols established within the standard operating procedures must be followed. Should a hazardous waste container appear to be leaking, swollen, or unstable in any way, it should be refused. Any disputes with the suspect generator which may arise from this type of situation should be handled by the undercover investigator.

Once the hazardous waste containers have been secured in the vehicle, they should be immediately transported to a predetermined facility for examination and sampling. It is recommended, for safety purposes, that the vehicle be followed by personnel trained in the handling of hazardous materials. Should the hazardous waste transportation team become disabled during transportation, it is essential that properly trained personnel be available for immediate assistance.

Extreme caution should be exhibited when the cargo area of the transport vehicle is opened for inspection or off-loading. The hazardous waste containers may have leaked liquids or fumes during their transportation. This may produce a flammable or poisonous vapor buildup within the cargo area. It is recommended that the cargo area of the vehicle be opened by properly trained and equipped personnel.

Examining Hazardous Waste

Once the hazardous waste containers have been transported to a secure facility, they should be examined and sampled (see Figure 47). If this location is a licensed treatment, storage, and disposal facility or a facility containing other hazardous wastes, every effort must be made to insure that no possibility of waste cross-contamination exists. This can be accomplished through proper hazardous waste segregation. The chemical evidence should be photographed and a full description of each container should be recorded. In addition, each container must be measured for the amount of hazardous waste present in the containers (see "Sampling for Criminal Evidence: Volume Reading Techniques" in Chapter 5).

Figure 47. These cyanide waste drums were obtained during a hazardous waste sting operation. Each drum has been sampled, measured and photographed. Note the lift gate-equipped undercover vehicle in the background.

Disposal

Hazardous waste sting operations of this type may continue for several months. During this period of time, numerous hazardous waste containers may have been obtained by the undercover team. It is essential that this hazardous waste be disposed of in a timely and proper manner.

It may be unreasonable to expect that these containers be maintained in their current condition until time of trial. Some hazardous wastes can break down into other chemical components and may become unstable over extended periods of time. In addition, the structural integrity of the containers may not be completely known. Should these containers begin to leak during storage, issues regarding public safety and site remediation costs may arise.

It is recommended that the environmental investigator meet with the prosecutor regarding this issue. It may be possible to obtain a court order authorizing the disposal of the hazardous waste drums prior to criminal charges being filed. If all reasonable measures have been taken to adequately preserve the rights and interests of any future defendants, the court may issue such an order. These reasonable measures should include split samples, a complete inventory of the containers and photographs.

A hazardous waste manifest should be utilized whenever the waste is brought to a treatment, storage or disposal facility. A copy of this manifest should be maintained in the investigative files.

The Investigative Files

Multiple defendant cases such as these can produce dozens of audio and video recordings, hundreds of photographs, and numerous analytical results. It is recommend that a separate investigative file be opened for each suspect generator and that the file contain, at a minimum, the following information:

1. Copies of all investigative reports.

2. Copies of all audio and videotapes. Each tape should be marked with the case number, date of recording, and the investigator's name.

3. Transcripts from all audiotapes.

4. Copies of all still photographs. Each photograph should be dated and marked with the case number and photographer's name.

5. Facility background information. This should include all information obtained through the examination of regulatory agency files.

6. Suspect background information. This should include photographs of the suspect, past criminal history information, motor vehicle information, and any other information that may be essential in the future identification, arrest, and prosecution of this individual.

7. Copies of chemical analytical results.

8. Records of any expenditures made during the course of the investigation.

9. Record of any court-ordered evidence destruction.

10. Copies of all manifests.

Appendix

STANDARD OPERATING PROCEDURES
ENVIRONMENTAL CRIME UNIT

"CRIME SCENES"

The following Standard Operating Procedures are designed to meet all requirements for emergency hazardous material response as set forth by the Local Emergency Planning Committee and all requirements set forth in S.A.R.A., TITLE III, 29 CFR 1910.120/146. SECTION 1 is a description of procedures to be followed at a hazardous waste/substance abandonment crime scene. SECTION 2 is a description of procedures to be followed at a facility where hazardous wastes/substances are suspected of being discharged on site and a search warrant or consent search is to be executed by Environmental Crime Unit personnel. *All hazardous waste/substance crime scenes are restricted to hazardous material trained personnel only.*

SECTION 1

CRIME SCENE PROCEDURES

ABANDONMENT OF HAZARDOUS WASTES/SUBSTANCES

I. NOTIFICATION

Environmental Crime Unit personnel will receive notification of a hazardous waste/substance abandonment crime scene via the Police Department Duty Officer. Two environmental crime unit detective s will be on 24-hour call at all times. Home telephone numbers and pager numbers for Environmental Crime Unit investigative personnel are to be listed with the Duty Officer. In accordance with 29 CFR 1910.120 (Buddy System), a minimum of two environmental crime unit detective s are to respond.

II. RESPONSE

Prior to arrival at the crime scene, an environmental crime unit detective will contact, via radio, the hazardous material response team members at the site and receive directions for a safe approach.

III. ARRIVAL

Upon arrival at the crime scene, one environmental crime unit detective will assume the role of crime-scene coordinator. Environmental crime unit detectives are to receive a briefing from the on-scene coordinator. All witnesses are to be interviewed prior to the site investigation team's entry into any declared Hot Zone.

IV. CRIME-SCENE COORDINATOR

It will be the crime-scene coordinator's responsibility to control all of the crime scene paperwork contained in the environmental crime unit's crime-scene packet. The following paperwork is to be completed during the crime-scene investigation:

1. On-site personnel list.
2. Container diagrams.
3. Crime-scene sketch.
4. Placards.

The crime-scene coordinator will be responsible for all decisions regarding the gathering of physical and chemical evidence. However, *the safety officer must give final approval for all activities conducted within the Hot Zone.* In addition, the crime-scene coordinator will be responsible for contacting laboratory and sampling team personnel.

V. COMMUNICATIONS

A two-way, throat-activated and intrinsically safe communication system will be utilized. Only those individuals entering the Hot Zone will be on the *throat activation* setting. The following personnel shall be on the communication system during the Hot Zone entry: safety officer, science officer, backup team members, and site-investigation team. All communication equipment is to be tested prior entering the Hot Zone.

VI. SITE INVESTIGATION TEAM (HOT ZONE)

The crime-scene coordinator and his or her partner will enter the Hot Zone *after* the safety officer has established the appropriate personal protection levels and back-up team. Photographs of the undisturbed scene are to be taken from outside of Hot Zone prior to entry.

A. Duties (Hot Zone):
1. Radiological survey.
2. LEL/O^2 readings.
3. Leak/spill check.
4. Container fuming check.
5. Container swelling check.
6. Container noise check.

    7. Signs of product crystallization.
    8. Note all markings.
    9. Note all labels.
  10. Note and cast all footprints.
  11. Note, caste and photograph all tire tracks.
  12. Note, collect and photograph any ground evidence.
  13. Note and photograph all DOT information.
  14. Note, dust, lift and photograph all fingerprints.
  15. Estimate gallonage.
  16. Sketch scene and containers.
  17. Placard and photograph containers.
  18. Open containers.
  19. Conduct field pH test.
  20. Repeat LEL/O^2 readings.
  21. Repeat radiological survey.
  22. Determine analytical parameters.
  23. Replace bung/lids (do not tighten).
  24. Photograph entire scene from all sides.

B. Equipment
    1. Appropriate chemical clothing.
    2. Appropriate boots.
    3. Appropriate gloves.
    4. One fully-charged S.C.B.A. (60-min. bottle).
    5. Non-sparking clip board.
    6. Pen.
    7. Bold marker.
    8. Placards.
    9. Duct Tape.
  10. LEL/O^2 meter.
  11. Radiological meter.
  12. pH paper and chart.
  13. Camera and flash.
  14. Evidence bags.
  15. Bung wrench.
  16. Knife (non-sparking).

VII. POST-SITE INVESTIGATION BRIEFING

  Upon exiting the Hot Zone, environmental crime unit detective s will follow all decontamination procedures as determined by the safety officer. After decontamination, a briefing will be conducted by the Crime-scene coordinator. The following personnel *must be in attendance*:

    1. Site safety officer
    2. Site science officer
    3. Sample team leader.

A. The following items will be determined at the briefing:
1. Sample team protection level.
2. Sampling equipment.
3. Sample points.
4. Backup team requirements.
5. Decontamination requirements.
6. Gallonage measurement.
7. Sample types:
    a. Metals.
    b. pH (electronic).
    c. Organics (volatile/semivolatile).
    d. Pensky-Martens Flash Point.
    e. Oil/Grease.
    h. Asbestos.
    i. Phenols.
    j. PCBs.
    k. T.C.L.P.
    l. Other.

VIII. POST-SAMPLING PROCEDURES

It is the responsibility of the crime-scene coordinator to record all gallonage readings as they are obtained by the sample team. Also, the crime-scene coordinator will observe the evidence chain-of-custody throughout the chemical evidence collection. The crime-scene coordinator will have photographs taken of *gallonage reading sticks* after the sample team has left the Hot Zone. The crime-scene coordinator will meet with the sample team leader and science officer to determine if the appropriate chemical evidence has been collected. The crime-scene coordinator will insure that all equipment and contaminated clothing have been properly removed from the crime scene. He or she will note and record the time at which the Crime Scene is closed.

The crime-scene coordinator shall maintain the investigation through its conclusion.

SECTION 2

CRIME-SCENE PROCEDURES

FACILITY SEARCH WARRANT OR CONSENT SEARCH

I. BRIEFING

A briefing shall be held, except when otherwise indicated, at least 24 hours prior to the execution of any and all environmental crime unit search warrants. The following groups shall be in attendance: environmental crime unit personnel, hazardous material response team personnel, sample team members, emergency medical team members (if required) and forensic chemists.

The crime-scene coordinator shall conduct the briefing. During the briefing the following items will be established:

1. Crime-scene coordinator.
2. Scene safety officer.
3. Scene science officer.
4. Site investigation team(s).
5. Facility location.
6. Type of industry.
7. Suspected chemicals/MSDS.
8. Suspected sample points.
9. Expected protection levels.
10. Equipment requirements.
11. Decontamination requirements.
12. Weather.
13. Site history.
14. Photographs.
15. Diagrams.
16. Medical requirements.
17. Review warrant.
18. Set staging area.
19. Set sample team(s).
20. Execution date & time.
21. Executive officer.

II. STAGING AREA

All search-warrant team members will assemble at the staging area. The crime-scene coordinator will insure that all personnel are present and will advise all search-warrant team members of any new information regarding the execution of the search warrant.

III. SEARCH WARRANT EXECUTION

At the previously-determined time the entire search-warrant team will enter the facility. The crime-scene coordinator and *uniformed personnel* will attempt to notify a facility representative of the search warrant's execution. All other personnel will remain with their vehicles until the proper parking and equipment-setup areas are established by the site safety officer.

IV. SITE INVESTIGATION TEAM(S)

After the vehicles and equipment have been properly stationed, the investigation team(s) will meet with the crime-scene coordinator and scene safety officer. The investigation team(s) will then be dispatched. Each investigation team shall include the following personnel:

1. One environmental crime unit detective.
2. One hazardous materials team member.

3. One sample team member.

4. One forensic chemist.

A. The *interior* site-investigation team will note the following:

    1. Waste-discharge points.

    2. Discharge pipes.

    3. Sinks.

    4. Sink elbows.

    5. Toilets.

    6. Floor drains.

    7. Holes in walls.

    8. Waste drums.

    9. Tanks.

    10. Raw product.

    11. Hoses.

    12. Sample points.

    13. Pumps.

    14. Sample types.

    15. Sample equipment needed.

    16. Safety equipment needed.

    17. Holes in floors.

B. The *exterior* site-investigation team will note the following:

    1. All storm drains.

    2. All sanitary pools/tanks.

    3. All piping.

    4. Raw-product storage areas.

    5. Waste storage areas.

    6. Safety equipment needed.

    7. Ground stains.

    8. Ground depressions.

    9. Sample points.

    10. Analytical parameters.

    11. Sampling devices required.

The detectives assigned to the interior and exterior site-investigation teams will insure that each sample point is placarded and photographed. The detectives will also insure that a complete inventory of raw product is conducted. If an area is located that appears to be contaminated with hazardous substances and/or hazardous wastes, to such an extent that it requires any level (A-C) of personal-protection equipment, the site investigation in that area is to cease immediately and the area reported to the crime-scene coordinator and safety officer. The crime-scene coordinator and the safety officer will then establish an appropriate plan to safely examine this area.

V. POST-INVESTIGATION BRIEFING

Upon completion of the above duties, the site-investigation team(s) will meet with the crime-scene coordinator, safety officer and science officer. The following items will be established at this Briefing:

    1. Sample team protection levels.

2. Sampling devices required.
3. Sample points.
4. Analytical parameters:
    a. Metals.
    b. pH (electronic).
    c. Organics (volatile/semivolatile).
    d. Pensky-Martens Flash Point.
    e. Oil/grease.
    f. Asbestos.
    g. Phenols.
    h. PCBs.
    i. T.C.L.P.
    j. Other.
5. Backup team requirements.
6. Decontamination requirements.
7. Gallonage measurements.
8. Communications.

Upon completion of the briefing, and prior to the collection of chemical evidence, the crime-scene coordinator will re-examine the site to assure that all appropriate sample points have been designated.

VI. CHEMICAL EVIDENCE COLLECTION

During the sampling procedures, the crime-scene coordinator, safety officer, and science officer shall remain together. The crime-scene coordinator will note each sample point and volumes (gallonage) in the crime scene records and complete a crime scene sketch. *The safety officer must give final approval for all activities conducted in any declared hot zone.* At the completion of the chemical evidence collection, the sample team leader will maintain the chain-of-custody for all chemical evidence. The crime-scene coordinator is to insure that the evidence chain-of-custody is kept in accordance with standard evidence collection procedures.

VII. EMPLOYEE IDENTIFICATION

Environmental crime unit detectives will attempt to identify as many employees as possible through personal interviews and the recording of employee license plate numbers. Names, addresses, dates of birth, job descriptions and length of employment are to be determined.

VIII. DYE TESTING

Dye testing of all suspect plumbing and piping will be conducted by two environmental crime unit detectives using vegetable dyes. The crime-scene coordinator will note in the crime-scene records the times, personnel, colors, origination, and discharge points.

IX. SITE CLEAN-UP

The crime-scene coordinator and safety officer will insure that all contaminated equipment and clothing is bagged and removed from the search warrant scene. He or she will also insure that all pools, tanks, and drums have been properly resealed and/or covered.

X. CLOSING OF THE CRIME SCENE

The crime-scene coordinator will receive, from the sample team leader, an inventory of all chemical evidence collected at the site. The crime-scene coordinator will issue a receipt for evidence removed (carbon copy made) to a representative of the facility. If no representative is available, the receipt shall be securely taped to an exterior door of the building. The crime-scene coordinator shall take custody of all film and photographs made during the execution of the search warrant.

The crime-scene coordinator is to insure that all search-warrant team personnel are accounted for and have exited the search-warrant site. He or she is to note the time that the crime scene is closed. The crime-scene coordinator shall maintain this investigation through its conclusion.

GLOSSARY

Acute Hazardous Wastes Those hazardous wastes that have proven to be fatal to humans or laboratory animals through inhalation or oral or dermal low-dosage exposure.

Bailer This device is normally used for sampling well-water. It consists of a container attached to a cable that is lowered into the well to retrieve a sample.

Ambient Air Any unconfined portion of the atmosphere: open air, surrounding air.

Asbestos A mineral fiber that can pollute air or water and cause cancer or asbestosis when inhaled. The EPA has banned or severely restricted its use in manufacturing and construction.

Baffle A flat board or plate, deflector, guide or similar device constructed or placed in a liquid containment system to cause more uniform flow velocities, to absorb energy, and to divert, guide, or agitate liquids.

CERCLA The Comprehensive Environmental Response, Compensation and Liability Act of 1980 (Superfund), as amended by the Superfund Amendment and Reauthorization Act (SARA) 1986.

Chain-of-Custody A system used to maintain the integrity of physical evidence. This may include physical possession, constant view, or secured and restricted access to the physical evidence.

Characteristic Hazardous Waste Any one of the four categories used in defining hazardous waste: ignitability, corrosivity, reactivity, and toxicity.

Chemical Analysis Request Sheet A document partially completed by the lead sampler which indicates the type or types of analysis to be conducted on the chemical evidence. This document accompanies the chemical evidence to the laboratory.

Coliwasa Tube Composite Liquid Waste Sampler is a device used to sample free-flowing liquids and slurries contained in drums, shallow tanks, pits, and similar containers. It is especially useful for sampling wastes that consist of several liquid layers.

Confined Space An area that is large enough and configured in such a way as to allow a person to enter and work. The area must have limited or

157

restricted means of entry or exit and is not designed for continuous employee occupancy.

Corrosivity A characteristic of hazardous waste which, when in an aqueous state, exhibits a pH less than or equal to 2 or greater than or equal to 12.5. Corrosive material corrodes steel at a rate greater than 6.35 mm per year at test temperature of 55° C.

Crime-Scene Coordinator The criminal investigator at an environmental crime scene who coordinates all evidence-gathering activities.

Cross Contamination A type of contamination caused by the introduction of part of one sample into a second sample during sampling, transportation and/or storage.

DOT Date A date that appears on certain hazardous material containers which indicates the month and year the container was tested for its integrity.

Digestion Procedure Introduction of an oxidizing acid solution into a sample prior to analysis.

Dipper A glass or plastic beaker clamped to the end of a telescoping pole that serves as the handle. A dipper samples liquids and free-flowing slurries.

Discharge Flow of surface water in a stream or canal or the outflow of ground water from a flowing artesian well, ditch, or spring. Can also apply to discharge of liquid effluent from a facility or of chemical emissions into the air through designated venting mechanisms.

Discharge Monitoring Report (DMR) Analytical reports which monitor the effluent discharge from a point source.

Disposal Final placement or destruction of toxic, radioactive, or other wastes; surplus or banned pesticides or other chemicals; polluted soils; or drums containing hazardous materials.

Drum Dolly A two wheeled device used to move heavy drums.

Drum Rings Ground-surface indentations and stains found in the shape of rings created by heavy and/or leaking drums.

Dye Test The use of vegetable dye to determine if two points are connected by a piping and/or plumbing system.

Dräeger-Tube Chemical test equipment which produces a color reaction when a specific contaminant is drawn through the tube.

Elute To remove, wash out or extract absorbed material from an absorbent by means of a solvent.

Emergency Planning and Community Right-To-Know Act (EPCRA) This 1986 Act establishes requirements for federal, state and local governments and industry regarding emergency planning and "community right-to-know" reporting on hazardous and toxic chemicals.

EPA ID Number The unique code number assigned to each generator, transporter, and treatment, storage, or disposal facility by regulating agencies to facilitate identification and tracking of chemicals or hazardous waste.

EP Toxicity Method of determining toxicity by a procedure that simulates leaching. If a certain concentration of a toxic substance can be leached from a waste, that waste is considered hazardous, i.e., "E P Toxic."

Extension Auger Consists of sharpened spiral blades attached to a hard metal extendible shaft. This device samples hard or packed solid wastes or soil.

Extremely Hazardous Substance Any of 406 chemicals identified by EPA as toxic, and listed under SARA Title III. The list is subject to periodic revision.

Fecal Coliform Bacteria Bacteria found in the intestinal tracts of mammals. Its presence in water or sludge is an indicator of pollution and possible contamination by pathogens.

Federal Hazard Communications Standard The occupational safety and health standard which addresses the issue of evaluating the potential hazards of chemicals in the work place and communicating that information to employees.

Field Blank A sample collected at specified frequencies normally used to detect sampling equipment contamination.

Flame Ionization Detector (FID) Chemical detector which detects the presence of organic compounds by using a hydrogen/air flame.

Flash Point The minimum temperature at which a liquid gives off a vapor in sufficient concentration to ignite when exposed to a flame or other ignition source.

Generator Any person who, by contract, agreement, or otherwise, arranged for disposal or treatment, or arranged with a transporter for disposal or treatment, of hazardous substances owned or possessed by such person, by any other party or entity, at any facility or incineration vessel owned or operated by another party or entity and containing such hazardous substances.

GC/MS Gas chromatography/mass spectrometer. An instrument used to detect the presence of, and determine the concentrations of, numerous volatile and semi-volatile organic chemical compounds in a sample.

Hazard Communication Standard An OSHA regulation that requires chemical manufacturers, suppliers, and importers to assess the hazards of the chemicals that they make, supply, or import, and to inform employers, customers, and workers of these hazards through Material Safety Data Sheets (MSDSs).

Hazardous Material A substance or material which has been determined by the Secretary of Transportation to be capable of posing an unreasonable risk to health, safety, and property when transported in commerce and which has been so designated.

Hazardous Substances Any substance defined as a hazardous substance under CERCLA, any biologic agent or other disease causing agent which after release into the environment and upon exposure will or may reasonably be anticipated to cause death, disease, behavioral abnormalities, cancer, genetic mutation, physiological malfunctions or physical deformation in a person or their offspring, any substance listed by the US Department of Transportation as a Hazardous Material or any hazardous waste.

Hazardous Waste By-products of society that can pose a substantial or potential hazard to human health or the environment when improperly managed. Possesses at least one of four characteristics (ignitability, corrosivity, reactivity, or toxicity), or appears on special EPA lists.

Hazardous Waste Manifest A document which is prepared for the purpose of tracking the shipment of hazardous wastes off the site of generation.

Hazardous Waste Manifest System Procedure in which hazardous wastes are identified and followed as they are produced, treated, transported, and disposed of by a series of permanent, linkable, descriptive documents (e.g., manifests). Commonly referred to as the cradle-to-grave system.

Holding-Time Requirements The recommended time period in which chemical evidence should be analyzed. The time period is measured from the time of collection to the time of analysis.

Hot Zone Area immediately surrounding a hazardous materials incident (including hazardous waste), extending far enough to prevent adverse effects from hazardous materials releases to personnel outside the zone.

ICP/AES Inductively coupled plasma/atomic emissions spectrometer, used to perform elemental analysis on samples.

Ignitability A hazardous waste characteristic. A liquid other than an aqueous solution is considered to be ignitable if it contains less than 24% Alcohol by volume and has a flash point less than 60° C (140° F). A nonliquid is considered ignitable if it is capable, under standard temperature and pressure, of causing fire through friction, absorption of moisture, or spontaneous chemical changes and, when ignited, burns so vigorously and persistently that it creates a hazard. A compressed gas is considered ignitable if it meets the criteria defined in 49 CFR 173.300. It is an oxidized as defined in 49 CFR 173.151.

Ignitability Test A test used to determine if a sample has the hazardous waste characteristic of ignitability (i.e., Pensky-Martens Closed Cup Tester).

Incident Command System (ICS) The organizational arrangement where in one person is in charge of an integrated, comprehensive emergency response organization and the emergency incident site, backed with resources, information, and advice by an emergency operations center.

Industrial Waste Unwanted materials from an industrial operation; may be liquid, sludge, solid, or hazardous waste.

Leaching The process by which soluble constituents are dissolved and filtered through the soil by a percolating fluid.

Leaching Pool A waste containment system designed in such a way as to allow its contents to leach into the soil.

LEL/O$_2$ Meter Lower explosive limit/oxygen meter which measures the concentration of a compound in the air below which the mixture will not catch on fire. This meter also measures the amount of oxygen present in the air.

Level "A" Protection Equipment Protection equipment that includes a positive pressure, full face-piece self-contained breathing apparatus (SCBA) or a positive pressure supplied air respirator with escape SCBA, totally encapsulating chemical protective suit, inner and outer chemical resistant gloves, and chemical resistant steel toed and shank boots. This level of protection is selected when the greatest level of skin, respiratory, and eye protection is required.

Level "B" Protection Equipment Protection equipment that includes a positive pressure, full face-piece self-contained breathing apparatus (SCBA), or a positive pressure supplied air respirator and escape SCBA, hooded chemical resistant clothing, inner and outer chemical resistant gloves and chemical resistant steel toe and shank boots. This level of protection is selected when the highest level of respiratory protection is necessary but a lesser level of skin protection is needed.

Level "C" Protection Equipment Protection equipment that includes a full-face or half mask, air purifying respirator, hooded chemical resistant clothing, inner and outer chemical resistant gloves, and chemical resistant steel toe and shank boots. This level of protection is selected when the concentration(s) and type(s) of airborne substance(s) are known and the criteria for using air purifying respirators are met.

Local Emergency Planning Committee (LEPC) A committee appointed by the state emergency response commission, as required by SARA, Title III, to formulate a comprehensive emergency plan for its jurisdiction.

Material Safety Data Sheet (MSDS) A compilation of information required under the OSHA Communication Standard on the identity of hazardous chemicals, health, and physical hazards, exposure limits, and precautions.

Chemical Buyers Directory A commercial directory indicating the names of chemical manufacturers and the chemicals that they produce.

OSHA The Occupational Safety and Health Administration.

Parts-Per-Billion (PPB) Unit commonly used to express the quantification of a substance in a sample.

Parts Per Million (PPM) Unit commonly used to express the quantification of a substance in a sample.

Personal-Protection Equipment (PPE) Safety equipment utilized by personnel working at a hazardous-materials incident or hazardous waste site. This equipment may include chemical clothing, gloves, boots, respirators, and/or self-contained breathing apparatus.

pH An expression of the intensity of the basic or acid condition of a liquid. The pH ranges from 0 to 14, with 0 being extremely acidic, 14 being extremely basic, and 7 being neutral. Natural waters usually have a pH between 6.5 and 8.5.

Photo-ionization Detector (PID) A chemical detector which consists of an ultraviolet lamp and ionization chamber. This device is used to detect the presence of organic compounds.

Placards A sign which represents the type of hazard of a particular hazardous material being offered or transported.

Point Source Means any discernible, confined and discrete conveyance, including but not limited to any pipe, ditch, channel, tunnel, conduit, well, discrete fissure, container, rolling stock, concentrated animal feeding operation, or vessel or other floating craft, from which pollutants are or may be discharged.

Poly Chlorinated Biphenyls (PCBs) These are chemicals that exhibit a high degree of chemical and biological stability, are lipid (fat) soluble and have a wide range of industrial uses. They are used as plasticizers, in hydraulic lubricants, and in electrical transformers. The oils are commonly straw colored. PCBs have been found in human blood plasma and fat tissues. They tend to accumulate in tissues and organs rich in lipids. In the U.S., PCBs are no longer produced or used in new equipment and existing transformers are highly regulated.

Ponar Grab Sampler This sampling device is used to obtain solid and slurry samples from the bottom of leaching pools. The device consists of two steel jaws, which close upon hitting the bottom of a pool.

Portable liquid sampler This sampling device allows for the automatic and timed sampling of waste streams.

Publicly-Owned Treatment Works (POTW) A publicly-owned sewer system that receives and treats wastes.

Press Wash A solvent mixture containing hazardous substances normally used to clean inks from printing presses.

RCRA Resource Conservation and Recovery Act of 1976. This act deals with the treatment, storage, transportation and disposal of hazardous wastes.

Safety Officer The individual at a hazardous-material incident or environmental crime scene who is responsible for establishing and supervising any required safety protocols.

Sampling Placard A sign used to identify individual sampling points through a systematic numbering system.

SARA Superfund Amendment and Reauthorization Act of 1986. Also known as Superfund.

Science Officer The individual at a hazardous-material incident or environmental crime scene who provides technical advice as to the chemicals present. This individual is normally a chemist.

Self-Audit Privilege A self-conducted environmental audit which systematically reviews the practices of a facility to detect non-compliance with certain environmental laws. Information derived from the self-audit is privileged information and, under some circumstances, may not be used against that facility in a regulatory or criminal proceeding.

Sewer A channel or conduit that carries wastewater and storm-water runoff from the source to a treatment plant or receiving stream. "Sanitary" sewers carry household, industrial, and commercial waste.

Solid Waste Nonliquid, nonsoluble materials ranging from municipal garbage to industrial wastes that contain complex and sometimes hazardous substances. Solid wastes also include sewage sludge, agricultural refuse, demolition wastes, and mining residues. Technically, solid waste also refers to liquids (including hazardous wastes) and gases in containers.

Specific gravity The ratio of the density of a substance to the density of some other substance (e.g., water) taken as a standard when both densities are obtained by weighing in air.

Split Samples The practice of taking an additional set of samples during a sampling event. As the sample is removed from the sampling device, 1/2 of the available sample is placed into a second sampling container.

Staging Area A prearranged area where personnel and equipment are temporarily maintained.

SW 846 The US Environmental Protection Agency's "Test Methods for Evaluating Solid Waste." This document established protocols for the sampling and analysis of hazardous waste.

Test Methods Approved procedures for measuring the presence and concentration of physical and chemical pollutants, evaluating properties such as the toxicity of chemical substances, or measuring the effects of substances under various conditions.

Total Metals An analytical procedure used to identify and quantify hazardous metallic elements such as mercury, chromium, cadmium, arsenic, and lead.

Total Petroleum Hydrocarbons (TPH) An analytical test used to identify the presence of petroleum in a sample (i.e., SW 846, Method 1664).

Trip Blank Sample containers of distilled water which accompany all sample containers to and from the field. Analysis of the trip blank will determine if any outside contamination or cross contamination occurred during handling and transportation.

Toxicity A characteristic of hazardous waste as determined by the Toxicity Characteristic Leaching Procedure.

Toxicity Characteristic Leaching Procedure (TCLP) A analytical extraction procedure conducted on liquid and solid samples to determine the hazardous waste characteristic of toxicity.

TSDF A Treatment, Storage and/or Disposal facility which handles hazardous wastes.

Volatile Organic Compound (VOC) Any organic compound that participates in atmospheric photochemical reactions except those designated by EPA as having negligible photochemical reactivity.

Waste Characterization The identification of chemical and microbiological constituents of a waste material.

Weighted Sampler Sampling device consisting of a weight, stopper, line and bottle. The line is used to raise, lower, and open the stopper allowing a sample to be taken. This device is used to sample liquids and free-flowing slurries.

X-ray Fluorescence Detector A detector used in determining the presence and quantification of certain metals (i.e., cadmium, lead).

NOTES

1. OSHA Hazardous Waste Operations and Emergency Response, 29 C.F.R. § 1910.120 (b) (li) (1996).
2. DOT Hazardous Material Table, 49 C.F.R. § 172.101 (1996).
3. OSHA Hazardous Waste Operations and Emergency Response, 29 C.F.R. § 1910.120 (3) (B) (1996).
4. OSHA Hazardous Waste Operations and Emergency Response, 29 C.F.R. § 1910.120 (3) (B) (1996).
5. Navigation and Navigable Waters, 33 U.S.C. § 1362 (14) (1996).
6. Navigation and Navigable Waters, 33 U.S.C. § 1342 (a) (1996).
7. OSHA Permit-required confined spaces, 29 C.F.R. § 1910.146 (1997).
8. EPA General Requirements, 40 C.F.R. § 262.20 (1997).
9. EPA Hazardous Chemical Reporting: Community Right-To-Know, 40 C.F.R. § 370.20 (1990).
10. EPA Emergency Planning and Notification, 40 C.F.R. § 355 Appendix A (1995).
11. EPA Reportable Quantities and Notification, 40 C.F.R. § 302.4 (1995).
12. OPD Chemical Buyers Directory. New York: Schnell, 1998.
13. EPA. *Test Methods for Evaluating Solid Waste* SW-846, (Washington DC, 1986) 9.2.
14. OSHA Appendix C, 29 C.F.R. § 1910.120 (2) (1996).
15. OSHA Hazardous Waste Operations and Emergency Response, 29 C.F.R. § 1910.120 (b) (2) (B) (1996).
16. OSHA Appendix C, 29 C.F.R. § 1910.120(6) (1996).
17. EPA. *Test Methods for Evaluating Solid Waste* SW-846, (Washington DC, 1986) 9.1
18. EPA. *Test Methods for Evaluating Solid Waste* SW-846, (Washington DC, 1995) 8.1
19. EPA. *Test Methods for Evaluating Solid Waste* SW-846, (Washington DC, 1995) 8.2
20. OSHA Hazard Communication, 29 C.F.R. § 1200 (b) (4) (ii) (1996).
21. DOT Hazardous Waste Manifest, 49 C.F.R. § 172.205 (e) (1996).
22. Linda Spahr, "Environmental Self-Audit Privilege: The Straw That Breaks the Back of Criminal Prosecutions," *Fordham Environmental Law Journal*, Vol. VII (1996): p.638.
23. OSHA Hazardous Waste Operations and Emergency Response, 29 C.F.R. § 1910.120 (L) (1) (1996).
24. OSHA Appendix C, 29 C.F.R. § 1910.120 (7) (1996).
25. Public Health and Welfare, 42 U.S.C. §§ 9604, 6927 (1996).
26. OSHA Hazardous Waste Operations and Emergency Response, 29 C.F.R. § 1910.120 (C) (7) (1996).

27. OSHA Appendix C, 29 C.F.R. § 1910.120 (7) (1996).

28. OSHA Hazardous Waste Operations and Emergency Response, 29 C.F.R. § 1910.120 (6) (I) (1996).

29. OSHA Hazardous Waste Operations and Emergency Response, 29 C.F.R. § 1910.120 (6) (I) (1996).

30. OSHA Hazardous Waste Operations and Emergency Response, 29 C.F.R. § 1910.120 (C) (7) (1996).

31. DOT Placards, 49 C.F.R. § 172.332 (c) (1997).

32. DOT Identification Codes for Packagings, 49 CFR § 178.502 (a) (1996).

33. EPA, *Test Methods for Evaluating Solid Waste* SW-846, (Washtington DC, 1995) 1.

34. EPA, *Test Methods for Evaluating Solid Waste* SW-846, (Washtington DC, 1995) 1.

35. EPA, *Test Methods for Evaluating Solid Waste* SW-846, (Washtington DC, 1995) 1.

36. EPA, *Test Methods for Evaluating Solid Waste* SW-846, (Washtington DC, 1986) 9.1.

37. EPA, *Test Methods for Evaluating Solid Waste* SW-846, (Washtington DC, 1994) 4.1.

38. EPA, *Test Methods for Evaluating Solid Waste* SW-846, (Washtington DC, 1995) 4.1.

39. EPA, *Test Methods for Evaluating Solid Waste* SW-846, (Washtington DC, 1994) 3.1.

40. EPA, *Test Methods for Evaluating Solid Waste* SW-846, Method 9010A, (Washtington DC, 1990) 6.1.

41. EPA, *Test Methods for Evaluating Solid Waste* SW-846, Method 1664 (Washtington DC, 1994) 6.1.

42. EPA, *Test Methods for Evaluating Solid Waste* SW-846, (Washtington DC, 1986) 9.1.

43. EPA, *Test Methods for Evaluating Solid Waste* SW-846, (Washtington DC, 1986) 9.2.2.7.

44. EPA, *Test Methods for Evaluating Solid Waste* SW-846, (Washtington DC, 1986) 9.2.2.7.

45. EPA, *Test Methods for Evaluating Solid Waste* SW-846, (Washtington DC, 1986) 9.2.2.7.

46. EPA, *Test Methods for Evaluating Solid Waste* SW-846, (Washtington DC, 1986) 9.2.2.7.

47. DOT Purpose and Scope, 49 CFR § 172.1 (1996).

48. EPA, Test Methods for Evaluating Solid Waste SW-846, (Washington DC, 1995).

49. EPA Toxicity Characteristic, 40 C.F.R. § 261.24 (1995).

50. EPA Toxicity Characteristic, 40 C.F.R. § 261.24 (1995).

51. EPA Corrosivity Characteristic, 40 C.F.R. § 261.22 (1995).

52. EPA Ignitability Characteristic, 40 C.F.R. § 261.21 (1995).

53. EPA Identification Numbers, 40 C.F.R. § 262.12 (a) (1996).

54. EPA Identification Numbers, 40 C.F.R. § 263.11 (a) (1996).

Table I 167

Table I
LIST OF HAZARDOUS SUBSTANCES AND STATUTORY AUTHORITY[1]

CERCLA Hazardous Substances"	CAS #	RCRA Waste[1]	RCRA Waste #	CLEAN WATER ACT[2]	CLEAN AIR ACT[3]
Acenaphthene	83329			*	
Acenaphthylene	208968			*	
Acetaldehyde	75070	*	U001	*	*
Acetaldehyde, chloro-	107200	*	P023		
Acetaldehyde, trichloro-	75876	*	U034		
Acetamide	60355				*
Acetamide, N-(aminothioxomethyl)-	591082	*	P002		
Acetamide, N-(4-ethoxyphenyl)-	62442	*	U187		
Acetamide, 2-fluro-	640197	*	P057		
Acetamide, N-9H-fluoren-2-yl-	53963	*	U005		*
Acetic acid	64197			*	
Acetic acid (2,4-dichlorophenoxy)- salts & esters	94757	*	U240	*	*
Acetic acid, Lead(2+)salt	301042	*	U144	*	
Acetic acid, thallium (1+) salt	563688	*	U214		
Acetic acid, (2,4,5-trichlorophenoxy)	93765	*	U232	*	
Acetic acid, ethyl ester	141786	*	U112		
Acetic acid, fluoro-,sodium salt	62748	*	P058		
Acetic acid anhydride	108247			*	
Acetone	67641	*	U002		
Acetone cyanohydrin	75865	*	P069	*	
Acetonitrile	75058	*	U003		*
Acetophenone	98862	*	U004		*
2-Acetylaminofluorene	53963	*	U005		*
Acetyl bromide	506967			*	
Acetyl chloride	75365	*	U006	*	

CERCLA Hazardous Substances[n]	CAS #	RCRA Waste[1]	RCRA Waste #	CLEAN WATER ACT[2]	CLEAN AIR ACT[3]
1-Acetyl-2-thiourea	591082	*	P002		
Acrolein	107028	*	P003	*	*
Acrylamide	79061	*	U007		*
Acrylic acid	79107	*	U008		*
Acrylonitrile	107131	*	U009	*	*
Adipic acid	124049			*	
Aldicarb	116063	*	P070		
Aldrin	309002	*	P004	*	
Allyl alcohol	107186	*	P005	*	
Allyl chloride	107051			*	*
Aluminum phosphide	20859738	*	P006		
Aluminum sulfate	10043013			*	
4-Aminobiphenyl	92671				*
5-(Aminomethyl)-3isoxazolol	2763964	*	P007		
4-Aminopyridine	504245	*	P008		
Amitrole	61825	*	U011		
Ammonia	7664417			*	
Ammonium acetate	631618			*	
Ammonium benzoate	1863634			*	
Ammonium bicarbonate	1066337			*	
Ammonium bichromate	7789095			*	
Ammonium bifluoride	1341497			*	
Ammonium bisulfite	10192300			*	
Ammonium carbamate	1111780			*	
Ammonium carbonate	506876			*	
Ammonium chloride	12125029			*	
Ammonium chromate	7788989			*	
Ammonium citrate, dibasic	3012655			*	

Table I   169

CERCLA Hazardous Substances††	CAS #	RCRA Waste[1]	RCRA Waste #	CLEAN WATER ACT[2]	CLEAN AIR ACT[3]
Ammonium fluoborate	13826830			*	
Ammonium fluoride	12125018			*	
Ammonium hydroxide	1336216			*	
Ammonium oxalate	6009707			*	
Ammonium picrate	131748	*	P009		
Ammonium silicofluoride	16919190			*	
Ammonium sulfamate	7773060			*	
Ammonium sulfide	12135761			*	
Ammonium sulfite	10196040			*	
Ammonium tartrate	14307438			*	
Ammonium thiocyanate	1762954			*	
Ammonium vanadate	7803556	*	P119		
Amyl acetate	628637			*	
Aniline	62533	*	U012	*	*
o-Anisidine	90040				*
Anthracene	120127			*	
Antimony	7440360			*	
Antimony compounds	N.A.			*	*
Antimony pentachloride	7647189			*	
Antimony potassium tartrate	28300745			*	
Antimony tribromide	7789619			*	
Antimony trichloride	10025919			*	
Antimony trifluoride	7783564			*	
Antimony trioxide	1309644			*	
Argentate(1-), bis(cyano-C)-potassium	506616	*	P099		
Aroclor 1016	12674112			*	*

CERCLA Hazardous Substances[n]	CAS #	RCRA Waste[1]	RCRA Waste #	CLEAN WATER ACT[2]	CLEAN AIR ACT[3]
Aroclor 1221	11104282			*	*
Aroclor 1232	11141165			*	*
Aroclor 1242	53469219			*	*
Aroclor 1248	12672296			*	*
Aroclor 1254	11097691			*	*
Aroclor 1260	11096825			*	*
Arsenic	7440382			*	*
Arsenic acid	1327522	*	P010		
Arsenic compounds (inorganic including arsine)	N.A.			*	*
Arsenic disulfide	1303328			*	
Arsenic pentoxide	1303282	*	P011	*	
Arsenic trichloride	7784341			*	
Arsenic trioxide	1327533	*	P012	*	
Arsenic trisulfide	1303339			*	
Arsine, diethyl-	692422	*	P038		
Arsinic acid, dimethyl-	75605	*	U136		
Arsonous dichloride, phenyl-	696286	*	P036		
Asbestos	1332214			*	*
Auramine	492808	*	U014		
Azaserine	115026	*	U015		
1H-Azepine-1-carbothioic acid, hexahydro-,S-ethyl ester (Molinate)	2212671	*	U365		
Aziridine	151564	*	P054		*
Aziridine, 2-methyl-	75558	*	P067		*
Azirino	50077	*	U010		
Barium cyanide	542621	*	P013	*	
Benz[j]aceanthrylene,1,2-dihydro-3-methyl-	56495	*	U157		

Table I 171

CERCLA Hazardous Substances[tt]	CAS #	RCRA Waste[1]	RCRA Waste #	CLEAN WATER ACT[2]	CLEAN AIR ACT[3]
Benz[c]acridine	225514	*	U016		
Benzal chloride	98873	*	U017		
Benzamide, 3,5-dichloro-N-(1,1-dimethyl-2-propynyl)-	23950585	*	U192		
Benz[a]anthracene	56553	*	U018	*	
Benz[a]anthracene, 7,12-dimethyl-	57976	*	U094		
Benzenamine	62533	*	U012	*	*
Benzenamine, 4,4'-carbonimidoylbis (N,N-dimethyl-	492808	*	U014		
Benzenamine, 4-chloro-	106478	*	P024		
Benzenamine, 4-chloro-2-methyl-, hydrochloride	3165933	*	U049		
Benzenamine, N,N-dimethyl-4-(phenylazo-)	60117	*	U093		*
Benzenamine, 2-methyl-	95534	*	U328		*
Benzenamine, 4-methyl-	106490	*	U353		
Benzenamine, 4,4'-methylenebis (2-chloro-	101144	*	U158		*
Benzenamine, 2-methyl-, hydrochloride	636215	*	U222		
Benzenamine, 2-methyl-5-nitro	99558	*	U181		
Benzenamine, 4-nitro-	100016	*	P077		
Benzene	71432	*	U109	*	*
Benzeneacetic acid, 4-chloro-*a*-(4-chlorophenyl)-*a*-hydroxy-,ethyl ester	510156	*	U038		*
Benzene, 1-bromo-4-phenoxy-	101553	*	U030	*	

CERCLA Hazardous Substances[n]	CAS #	RCRA Waste[1]	RCRA Waste #	CLEAN WATER ACT[2]	CLEAN AIR ACT[3]
Benzenebutanoic acid, 4-[bis(2-chloroethyl) amino]-	305033	*	U035		
Benzene, chloro-	108907	*	U037	*	*
Benzene, chloromethyl-	100447	*	P028	*	*
Benzenediamine, ar-methyl-	95807	*	U221		*
1,2- Benzenedicarboxylic acid, dioctyl ester	117840	*	U107	*	
1,2- Benzenedicarboxylic acid, bis (2-ethylhexyl)ester	117817	*	U028	*	*
1,2- Benzenedicarboxylic acid, dibutyl ester	84742	*	U069	*	*
1,2- Benzenedicarboxylic acid, diethyl ester	84662	*	U088	*	
1,2-Benzenedicarboxylic acid, dimethyl ester	131113	*	U102	*	*
Benzene, 1,2-dichloro-	95501	*	U070	*	
Benzene, 1,3-dichloro-	541731	*	U071	*	
Benzene, 1,4-dichloro-	106467	*	U072	*	*
Benzene, 1,1'-(2,2-dichloroethyl-idene)bis[4-chloro-	72548	*	U060	*	
Benzene, dichloromethyl-	98873	*	U017		
Benzene, 1,3-diisocyanatomethyl-	91087	*	U223		*
Benzene, dimethyl-	1330207	*	U239	*	*
Benzene, m-dimethyl-	108383				*
Benzene, o-dimethyl-	95476				*
Benzene, p-dimethyl-	106423				*
1,3-Benzenediol	108463	*	U201	*	
1,2-Benzenediol,4-[1-hydroxy-2-(methylamino)ethyl]-	51434	*	P042		

Table I 173

CERCLA Hazardous Substances[n]	CAS #	RCRA Waste[1]	RCRA Waste #	CLEAN WATER ACT[2]	CLEAN AIR ACT[3]
Benzeneethanamine, alpha, alpha-dimethyl-	122098	*	P046		
Benzene, hexachloro-	118741	*	U127	*	*
Benzene, hexahydro-	110827	*	U056	*	
Benzene, hydroxy-	108952	*	U188	*	*
Benzene, methyl-	108883	*	U220	*	*
Benzene, 2-methyl-1,3-dinitro-	606202	*	U106	*	
Benzene, 1-methyl-2,4-dinitro-	121142	*	U105	*	*
Benzene, (1-methylethyl)-	98828	*	U055		*
Benzene, nitro-	98953	*	U169	*	*
Benzene, pentachloro-	608935	*	U183		
Benzene, pentachloronitro-	82688	*	U185		*
Benzenesulfonic acid chloride	98099	*	U020		
Benzenesulfonyl chloride	98099	*	U020		
Benzene, 1,2,4,5-tetrachloro-	95943	*	U207		
Benzenethiol	108985	*	P014		
Benzene, 1,1'-(2,2,2-tri- chloro-ethylidene)bis[4-chloro-	50293	*	U061	*	
Benzene, 1,1'-(2,2,2-trichloro-ethylidene)bis[4-methoxy-	72435	*	U247	*	*
Benzene, (trichloromethyl)-	98077	*	U023		*
Benzene, 1,3,5-trinitro-	99354	*	U234		
Benzidine	92875	*	U021	*	*
1,2-Benzisothiazol-3(2H)-one,1,1-dioxide	81072	*	U202		
Benzo[a]anthracene	56553	*	U018	*	
Benzo[b]fluorathene	205992			*	
Benzo[k]fluorathene	207089			*	

CERCLA Hazardous Substances[ft]	CAS #	RCRA Waste[1]	RCRA Waste #	CLEAN WATER ACT[2]	CLEAN AIR ACT[3]
Benzo[j,k]fluorene	206440	*	U120	*	
1,3-Benzodioxol-4-ol, 2,2-dimethyl- (Bendiocarb phenol)	22961826	*	U364		
1,3-Benzodioxol-4-ol, 2,2-dimethyl- methyl carbamate (Bendiocarb)	22781233	*	U278		
1,3-Benzodioxole, 5-)1-propenyl)-	120581	*	U141		
1,3-Benxodioxole, 5-(2-propenyl)-	94597	*	U203		
1,3-Benzodioxole, 5-propyl-	94586	*	U090		
7-Benzofuranol, 2,3-dihydro-2,2- dimethyl- (Carbofuran phenol)	1563388	*	U367		
Benzoic acid	65850			*	
Benzoic acid, 2-hydroxy-,compd. with(3aS-cis)-1,2,3,3a,8,8a-hexa- hydro-1,3a,8-trimethylpyrrolo[2,3-*b*]indol-5-yl methylcarbamate ester (1:1)(Physostigmine salicylate)	57647	*	P188		
Benzonitrile	100470			*	
Benzo [rst]pentaphene	189559	*	U064		
Benzo [ghi]perylene	191242			*	
2H-1-Benzopyran-2-one,4-hydroxy- 3-(3-oxo-1-phenyl-butyl)-, & salts, when present at concentrations greater than 0.3%	81812	*	P001		
Benzo[a]pyrene	50328	*	U022	*	
3,4-Benzopyrene	50328	*	U022	*	
p-Benzoquinone	106514	*	U197		*
Benzotrichloride	98007	*	U023		*
Benzoyl chloride	98884			*	
1,2-Benzphenanthrene	218019	*	U050	*	

Table I   175

CERCLA Hazardous Substances[tt]	CAS #	RCRA Waste[1]	RCRA Waste #	CLEAN WATER ACT[2]	CLEAN AIR ACT[3]
Benzyl chloride	100447	*	P028	*	*
Beryllium Compounds	N.A.			*	*
Beryllium chloride	7787475			*	
Beryllium fluoride	7787497			*	
Beryllium nitrate	13597994			*	
Beryllium powder	7440417	*	P015	*	*
alpha-BHC	319846			*	
beta-BHC	319857			*	
delta-BHC	319868			*	
y-BHC	58899	*	U129	*	*
2,2'-Bioxirane	1464535	*	U085		
(1,1'-Biphenyl)-4,4'diamine	92875	*	U021	*	
[1,1'-Biphenyl]-4,4'diamine,3,3' dichloro-	91941	*	U073	*	
[1,1'-Biphenyl]-4,4'-diamine,3,3' dimethoxy-	119904	*	U091		
[1,1'-Biphenyl]-4,4'diamine,3,3- dimethyl-	119937	*	U095		
Biphenyl	92524				*
Bis (2-chloroethyl) ether	111444	*	U025	*	
Bis (2-chloroethoxy) methane	111911	*	U024	*	
Bis(dimethylthiocarbamoyl) sulfide (Tetramethylthiuram monosulfide)	97745	*	U401		
Bis (2-ethylhexyl)phthalate	117817	*	U028	*	
Bromoacetone	598312	*	P017		
Bromoform	75252	*	U225	*	
4-Bromophenyl phenyl ether	101553	*	U030	*	
Brucine	357573	*	P018		
1,3-Butadiene, 1,1,2,3,4,4-hexa- chloro-	87683	*	U128	*	

CERCLA Hazardous Substances"	CAS #	RCRA Waste[1]	RCRA Waste #	CLEAN WATER ACT[2]	CLEAN AIR ACT[3]
1,3-Butadiene	106990				*
1-Butanamine, N-butyl-N-nitroso-	924163	*	U172		
1-Butanol	71363	*	U031		
2-Butanone	78933	*	U159		*
2-Butanone peroxide	1338234	*	U160		
2-Butanone, 3,3-dimethyl-1-(methylthio)-,O[(methylamino) carbonyl] oxime	39196184	*	P045		
2-Butenal	123739 4170303	*	U053	*	
2-Butene, 1,4-dichloro-	764410	*	U074		
2-Butenoic acid, 2-methyl-,7[[2,3-dihydroxy-2-(1-methoxyethyl)-3-methyl-1-oxobutoxy]methyl]-2,3,5, 7a-tetrahydro-1H-pyrrolizin-1-yl ester,[1S-[1alpha(Z),7(2S*,3R*), 7aalpha]]-	303344	*	U143		
Butyl acetate	123864			*	
iso-Butyl acetate	110190				
sec-Butyl acetate	105464				
tert-Butyl acetate	540885				
n-Butyl alcohol	71363	*	U031		
Butylamine	109739			*	
iso-Butylamine	78819				
sec-Butylamine	513495139 52846				
tert-Butylamine	75649				
Butyl benzyl phthalate	85687			*	
η-Butyl phthalate	84742	*	U069	*	*

Table I 177

CERCLA Hazardous Substances[tt]	CAS #	RCRA Waste[1]	RCRA Waste #	CLEAN WATER ACT[2]	CLEAN AIR ACT[3]
Butyric acid	107926			*	
iso-Butyric acid	79312				
Cacodylic acid	75605	*	U136		
Cadmium	7440439			*	
Cadmium acetate	543908			*	
Cadmium Compounds	N.A.			*	*
Cadmium bromide	7789426			*	
Cadmium chloride	10108642			*	
Calcium arsenate	7778441			*	
Calcium arsenite	52740166			*	
Calcium carbide	75207			*	
Calcium chromate	13765190	*	U032	*	
Calcium cyanamide	156627				*
Calcium cyanide	592018	*	P021	*	
Calcium cyanide Ca(CN)2	592018	*	P021	*	
Calcium dodecylbenzenesulfonate	26264062			*	
Calcium hypochlorite	7778543			*	
Camphene, octachloro-	8001352	*	P123	*	*
Caprolactam	105602				*
Captan	133062			*	*
Carbamic acid, butyl-, 3-iodo-2-propynyl ester (3-iodo-2-propynyl n-butylcarbamate)	55406536	*	U375		
Carbamic acid, [1-[(butylamino) carbonyl]-1H-benzimidazol-2-yl, methyl ester (Benomyl)	17804352	*	U271		
Carbamic acid, 1H-benzimidazol-2-yl,methyl ester (Carbendazim)	10605217	*	U372		

CERCLA Hazardous Substances"	CAS #	RCRA Waste[1]	RCRA Waste #	CLEAN WATER ACT[2]	CLEAN AIR ACT[3]
Carbamic acid, (3-chlorophenyl)-, 4-chloro-2-butynyl ester (Barban)	101279	*	U280		
Carbamic acid, [(dibutylamino)thio] methyl-,2,3-dihydro-2,2-dimethyl-7-benzofuranyl ester (Carbosulfan)	55285148	*	P189		
Carbamic acid, dimethyl-,1-[(di-methylamino)carbonyl]-5-methyl-1H-pyrazol-3-yl ester (Dimetilan)	644644	*	P191		
Carbamic acid, dimethyl-,3-methyl-1-(1-methylethyl)-1H-pyrazol-5-yl ester (Isolan)	119380	*	P192		
Carbamic acid, ethyl ester	51796	*	U238		*
Carbamic acid, methylnitroso-, ethyl ester	615532	*	U178		
Carbamic acid, methyl-,3-methyl-phenyl ester (Metolcarb)	1129415	*	P190		
Carbamic acid, [1,2-phenylenebis (iminocarbonothlioyl)]bis-,dimethyl ester (Thiophanate-methyl)	23564058	*	U409		
Carbamic acid, phenyl-,1-methyl-ethyl ester (Propham)	122429	*	U373		
Carbamic chloride, dimethyl-	79447	*	U097		*
Carbamodithioic acid, 1,2-ethane-diylbis, salts & esters	111546	*	U114		

Table I 179

CERCLA Hazardous Substances[π]	CAS #	RCRA Waste[1]	RCRA Waste #	CLEAN WATER ACT[2]	CLEAN AIR ACT[3]
Carbamodithioic acid, dibutyl, sodium salt (Sodium dibutyldithiocarbamate)	136301	*	U379		
Carbamodithioic acid, diethyl-, 2-chloro-2-propenyl ester (Sulfallate)	95067	*	U277		
Carbamodithioic acid, diethyl-, sodium salt (Sodium diethyldithio-carbamate)	148185	*	U381		
Carbamodithioic acid, dimethyl, potassium salt (Potassium dimethyl-dithiocarbamate)	128030	*	U383		
Carbamodithioic acid, dimethyl-, sodium salt (Sodium dimethyldithio-carbamate)	128041	*	U382		
Carbamodithioic acid, dimethyl-, tetraanhydrosulfide with orthothio-selenious acid (Selenium, tetrakis (dimethyldithiocarbamate))	144343	*	U376		
Carbamodithioic acid, (hydroxy-methyl)methyl-, monopotassium salt (Potassium n-hydroxymethyl-n-methyldithiocarbamate)	51026289	*	U378		
Carbamodithioic acid, methyl,-monopotassium salt (Potassium n-methyldithiocarbamate)	137417	*	U377		
Carbamodithioic acid, methyl-, monosodium salt (Metam Sodium)	137428	*	U384		

CERCLA Hazardous Substances[tt]	CAS #	RCRA Waste[1]	RCRA Waste #	CLEAN WATER ACT[2]	CLEAN AIR ACT[3]
Carbamothioic acid, bis(1-metyhl-ethyl)- S(2,3-dichloro-2-propenyl) ester	2303164	*	U062		
Carbamothioic acid, bis(1-methyl-ethyl)-, S(2,3,3-trichloro-2-propenyl) ester (Triallate)	2303175	*	U389		
Carbamothioic acid, bis(2-methyl-propyl)-,S-ethyl ester (Butylate)	2008415	*	U392		
Carbamothioic acid, butylethyl-, S-propyl ester (Pebulate)	1114712	*	U391		
Carbamothioic acid, cyclohexyl-ethyl-,S-ethyl ester (Cycloate)	1134232	*	U386		
Carbamothioic acid, dipropyl-, S-ethyl ester (EPTC)	759944	*	U390		
Carbamothioic acid, dipropyl-, S-(phenylmethyl) ester (Prosulfocarb)	52888809	*	U387		
Carbamothioic acid, dipropyl-, S-propyl ester (Vernolate)	1929777	*	U385		
Carbaryl	63252			*	*
Carbofuran	1563662			*	
Carbon disulfide	75150	*	P022	*	*
Carbon oxyfluoride	353504	*	U033		
Carbonic acid, dithallium (1+) salt	6533739	*	U215		
Carbonic dichloride	75445	*	P095	*	*
Carbonic difluoride	353504	*	U033		
Carbonochloridic acid, methyl ester	79221	*	U156		
Carbon tetrachloride	56235	*	U211	*	*

Table I 181

CERCLA Hazardous Substances[n]	CAS #	RCRA Waste[1]	RCRA Waste #	CLEAN WATER ACT[2]	CLEAN AIR ACT[3]
Carbonyl sulfide	463581				*
Catechol	120809				*
Chloral	75876	*	U034		
Chloramben	133904				*
Chlorambucil	305033	*	U035		
Chlordane	57749	*	U036	*	*
CHLORDANE (TECHNICAL MIXTURE AND METABOLITES)	57749	*	U036	*	*
Chlordane, alpha & gamma isomers	57749	*	U036	*	*
CHLORINATED BENZENES	N.A.			*	
Chlorinated camphene	8001352	*	P123	*	*
CHLORINATED ETHANES	N.A.			*	
CHLORINATED NAPHTHALENE	N.A.			*	
CHLORINATED PHENOLS	N.A.			*	
Chlorine	7782505			*	*
Chlornaphazine	494031	*	U026		
Chloroacetaldehyde	107200	*	P023		
Chloroacetic acid	79118				*
2-Chloroacetophenone	532274				*
CHLOROALKYL ETHERS	N.A.			*	
p-Chloroaniline	106478	*	P024		
Chlorobenzene	108907	*	U037	*	*
Chlorobenzilate	510156	*	U038		*
4-Chloro-m-cresol	59507	*	U039	*	
p-Chloro-m-cresol	59507	*	U039	*	
Chloroethane	75003			*	*
Chlorodibromomethane	124481			*	
1-Chloro-2,3-epoxypropane	106898	*	U041	*	*

CERCLA Hazardous Substances[tt]	CAS #	RCRA Waste[1]	RCRA Waste #	CLEAN WATER ACT[2]	CLEAN AIR ACT[3]
2-Chloroethyl vinyl ether	110758	*	U042	*	
Chloroform	67663	*	U044	*	*
Chloromethane	74873	*	U045	*	*
Chloromethyl methyl ether	107302	*	U046		*
beta-Chloronaphthalene	91587	*	U047	*	
2-Chloronaphthalene	91587	*	U047	*	
2-Chlorophenol	95578	*	U048	*	
o-Chlorophenol	95578	*	U048	*	
4-Chlorophenyl phenyl ether	7005723			*	
1-(o-Chlorophenyl)thiourea	5344821	*	P026		
Chloroprene	126998				*
3-Chloropropionitrile	542767	*	P027		
Chlorosulfonic acid	7790945			*	
4-Chloro-o-toluidine, hydrochloride	3165993	*	U049		
Chlorpyrifos	2921882			*	
Chromic acetate	1066303			*	
Chromic acid	11115745			*	
Chromic acid H2CrO4, calcium salt	13765190	*	U032	*	
Chromic sulfate	10101538			*	
Chromium	7440473			*	
Chromium Compounds	N.A.			*	*
Chromous chloride	10049055			*	
Chrysene	218019	*	U050	*	
Cobalt Compounds	N.A.				*
Cobaltous bromide	7789437			*	
Cobaltous formate	544183			*	
Cobaltous sulfamate	14017415			*	
Coke Oven Emmissions	N.A.				*

Table I 183

CERCLA Hazardous Substances[n]	CAS #	RCRA Waste[1]	RCRA Waste #	CLEAN WATER ACT[2]	CLEAN AIR ACT[3]
Copper	7440508			*	
Copper and Compounds	N.A.			*	
Copper, bis(dimethylcarbamodi-thioato-S,S')-(Copper dimethyldithiocarbamate)	137291	*	U393		
Copper cyanide	544923	*	P029		
Copper cyanide CuCN	544923	*	P029		
Coumaphos	56724			*	
Creosote	8001589	*	U051		
Cresols (isomers and mixture)	1319773	*	U052	*	*
m-Cresol	108394				*
o-Cresol	95487				*
p-Cresol	106445				*
Cresylic acid (isomers and mixture)	1319773	*	U052	*	*
m-Cresylic acid	108394				*
o-Cresylic acid	95487				*
p-Cresylic acid	106445				*
Crotonaldehyde	123739	*	U053	*	
Cumene	98828	*	U055		*
Cupric acetate	142712			*	
Cupric acetoarsenite	12002038			*	
Cupric chloride	7447394			*	
Cupric nitrate	3251238			*	
Cupric oxalate	5893663			*	
Cupric sulfate	7758987			*	
Cupric sulfate, ammoniated	10380297			*	
Cupric tartrate	815827			*	
Cyanide Compounds	N.A.			*	*
CYANIDES	N.A.			*	*

CERCLA Hazardous Substances[††]	CAS #	RCRA Waste[1]	RCRA Waste #	CLEAN WATER ACT[2]	CLEAN AIR ACT[3]
Cyanides (soluble salts and complexes) not otherwise specified	57125	*	P030		
Cyanogen	460195	*	P031		
Cyanogen Bromide	506683	*	U246		
Cyanogen Bromide (CN)Br	506683	*	U246		
Cyanogen chloride	506774	*	P033	*	
Cyanogen chloride (CN)Cl	506774	*	P033	*	
2,5-Cyclohexadiene-1,4-dione	106514	*	U197		*
Cyclohexane	110827	*	U056	*	
Cyclohexane, 1,2,3,4,5,6-hexa-chloro-,(1α,2α,3β,4α,5α,6β)-	58899	*	U129	*	*
Cyclohexanone	108941	*	U057		
2-Cyclohexyl-4,6-dinitrophenol	131895	*	P034		
1,3-Cyclopentadiene, 1,2,3,4,5,5-hexachloro-	77474	*	U130	*	*
Cyclophosphamide	50180	*	U058		
2,4-D Acid	94757	*	U240	*	*
2,4-D Ester	94111 94791 94804 1320189 1928387 1928616 1929733 2971382 25168267 53467111			*	
2,4-D salts and esters	94757	*	U240	*	*
Daunomycin	20830813	*	U059		

Table I   185

CERCLA Hazardous Substances[tt]	CAS #	RCRA Waste[1]	RCRA Waste #	CLEAN WATER ACT[2]	CLEAN AIR ACT[3]
DDD	72548	*	U060	*	
4,4'DDD	72548	*	U060	*	
DDE	72559			*	*
4,4'-DDE	72559			*	*
DDE[b]	3547044				*
DDT	50293	*	U061	*	
4,4'-DDT	50293	*	U061	*	
DDT AND METABOLITES	N.A.			*	
DEHP	117817	*	U028	*	*
Diallate	2303164	*	U062		
Daizinon	333415			*	
Diazomethane	334883				*
Dibenz[a,h]anthracene	53703	*	U063	*	
1,2:5,6-Dibenzanthracene	53703	*	U063	*	
Dibenzo[a,h]anthracene	53703	*	U063	*	
Dibenz[a,i]pyrene	189559	*	U064		
Dibenzofuran	132649				*
1,2-Dibromo-3-chloropropane	96128	*	U066		*
Dibromoethane	106934	*	U067	*	*
Dibutyl phthalate	84742	*	U069	*	*
Di-n-butyl phthalate	84742	*	U069	*	*
Dicamba	1918009			*	
Dichlobenil	1194656			*	
Dichlone	117806			*	
Dichlorobenzene	25321226			*	
1,2-Dichlorobenzene	95501	*	U070	*	
1,3-Dichlorobenzene	541731	*	U071	*	
1,4-Dichlorobenzene	106467	*	U072	*	*

CERCLA Hazardous Substances[n]	CAS #	RCRA Waste[1]	RCRA Waste #	CLEAN WATER ACT[2]	CLEAN AIR ACT[3]
m-Dichlorobenzene254q1t6q15	541731	*	U071	*	
o-Dichlorobenzene	95501	*	U70	*	
p-Dichlorobenzene	106467	*	U072	*	*
DICHLOROBENZIDINE	N.A.			*	
3,3'-Dichlorobenzidine	91941	*	U073	*	*
Dichlorobromomethane	75274			*	
1,4-Dichloro-2-butene	764410	*	U074		
Dichlorodifluoromethane	75718	*	U075		
1,1-Dichloroethane	75343	*	U076	*	*
1,2-Dichloroethane	107062	*	U077	*	*
1,1-Dichloroethylene	75354	*	U078	*	*
1,2-Dichloroethylene	156605	*	U079	*	
Dichloroethyl ether	111444	*	U025	*	*
Dichloroisopropyl ether	108601	*	U027	*	
Dichloromethane	75092	*	U080	*	*
Dichloromethoxy ethane	111911	*	U024	*	
Dichloromethyl ether	542881	*	P016		*
2,4-Dichlorophenol	120832	*	U081	*	
2-6-Dichlorophenol	87650	*	U082		
Dichlorophenylarsine	696286	*	P036		
Dichloropropane	26638197			*	
1,1-Dichloropropane	78999				
1,3-Dichloropropane	142289				
1,2-Dichloropropane	78875	*	U083	*	*
Dichloropropane-Dichloropropene (mixture)	8003198			*	
Dichloropropene	26952238			*	
2,3-Dichloropropene	78886				

Table I   187

CERCLA Hazardous Substances[tt]	CAS #	RCRA Waste[1]	RCRA Waste #	CLEAN WATER ACT[2]	CLEAN AIR ACT[3]
1,3-Dichloropropene	542756	*	U084	*	*
2,2-Dichloropropionic acid	75990			*	
Dichlorvos	62737			*	*
Dicofol	115322			*	
Dieldrin	60571	*	P037	*	
1,2:3,4-Diepoxybutane	1464535	*	U085		
Diethanolamine	111422				*
Diethylamine	109897			*	
N,N-Diethylaniline	91667				*
Diethylarsine	692422	*	P038		
1,4-Diethylenedioxide	123911	*	U108		*
1,4- Diethlenoxide	123911	*	U108		*
Diethylhexyl phthalate	117817	*	U028	*	*
N,N'-Diethylhydrazine	1615801	*	U086		
O,O-Diethyl S-methyl dithiophos- phate	3288582	*	U087		
Diethyl-p-nitrophenyl phosphate	311455	*	P041		
Diethyl phthalate	84662	*	U088	*	
O,O-Diethyl O-pyrazinyl phosphorothioate	297972	*	P040		
Diethylstilbestrol	56531	*	U089		
Diethyl sulfate	64675				*
Dihydrosafrole	94586	*	U090		
3,3'-Dimethoxybenzidine	119904	*	U091		*
Dimethylamine	124403	*	U092	*	
Dimethyl aminoazobenzene	60117	*	U093		*
p-Dimethylaminoazobenzene	60117	*	U093		*
N,N-Dimethylaniline	121697				*

Environmental Crime

CERCLA Hazardous Substances[π]	CAS #	RCRA Waste[1]	RCRA Waste #	CLEAN WATER ACT[2]	CLEAN AIR ACT[3]
7,12-Dimethylbenz[a]anthracene	57976	*	U094		
3,3'-Dimethylbenzidine	119937	*	U095		*
alpha,alpha-Dimethylbenzylhydro-peroxide	80159	*	U096		
Dimethylcarbamoyl chloride	79447	*	U097		*
Dimethylformamide	68122				*
1,1-Dimethylhydrazine	57147	*	U098		*
1,2-Dimethylhydrazine	540738	*	U099		
alpha,alpha-Dimethylphene-thylamine	122098	*	P046		
2,4-Dimethylphenol	105679	*	U101	*	
Dimethyl phthalate	131113	*	U102	*	*
Dimethyl sulfate	77781	*	U103		*
Dinitrobenzene (mixed)	25154545			*	
m-Dinitrobenzene	99650				
o-Dinitrobenzene	528290				
p-Dinitrobenzene	100254				
4,6-Dinitro-o-cresol, and salts	534521	*	P047	*	*
Dinitrophenol	25550587			*	
2,5-Dinitrophenol	329715				
2,6-Dinitrophenol	573568				
2,4-Dinitrophenol	51285	*	P048	*	*
Dinitrotoluene	25321146			*	
3,4-Dinitrotoluene	610399				
2,4-Dinitrotoluene	121142	*	U105	*	*
2,6-Dinitrotoluene	606202	*	U106	*	
Dinoseb	88857	*	P020		
Di-n-octyl phthalate	117840	*	U107	*	
1,4-Dioxane	123911	*	U108		*

Table I 189

CERCLA Hazardous Substances[tt]	CAS #	RCRA Waste[1]	RCRA Waste #	CLEAN WATER ACT[2]	CLEAN AIR ACT[3]
DIPHENYLHYDRAZINE	N.A.			*	
1,2-Diphenyl- hydrazine	122667	*	U109	*	*
Diphosphoramide octamethyl-	152169	*	P085		
Diphosphoric acid, tetraethyl ester	107493	*	P111	*	
Dipropylamine	142847	*	U110		
Di-n-propylnitrosamine	621647	*	U111	*	
Diquat	85007			*	
Disulfoton	298044	*	P039	*	
Dithiobiuret	541537	*	P049		
1,3-Dithiolane-2-carboxaldehyde, 2,4-dimethyl-, O-[(methyl-amino)carbonyl]oxime (Tirpate)	26419738	*	P185		
Diuron	330541			*	
Dodecylbenzenesulfonic acid	27176870			*	
Endosulfan	115297	*	P050	*	
alpha-Endosulfan	959988			*	
beta-Endosulfan	33213659			*	
ENDROSULFAN AND METABOLITES	N.A.			*	
Endrosulfan sulfate	1031078			*	
Endothall	145733	*	P088		
Endrin	72208	*	P051	*	
Endrin aldehyde	7421934			*	
Endrin and metabolites	72208	*	P051	*	
Epichlorohydrin	106898	*	U041	*	*
Epinephrine	51434	*	P042		
1,2-Epoxybutane	106887				*
Ethanal	75070	*	U001	*	*
Ethanamine, N-ethyl-N-nitroso-	55185	*	U174		

CERCLA Hazardous Substances[n]	CAS #	RCRA Waste[1]	RCRA Waste #	CLEAN WATER ACT[2]	CLEAN AIR ACT[3]
1,2-Ethanediamine, N,N-dimethyl-N'-2-pyridinyl-N'-2-pyridinyl-N'-(2-thienylmethyl)-	91805	*	U155		
Ethane, 1,2-dibromo	106934	*	U067	*	*
Ethane, 1,1-dichloro	75343	*	U076	*	*
Ethane, 1,2-dichloro	107062	*	U077	*	*
Ethanedinitrile	460195	*	P031		
Ethane, hexachloro-	67721	*	U131	*	*
Ethan, 1,1'-[methylenebis(oxy)]bis (2-chloro-	111911	*	U024	*	
Ethane, 1,1'-oxybis-	60297	*	U117		
Ethane, 1,1'-oxybis[2-chloro-	111444	*	U025	*	*
Ethan, pentachloro-	76017	*	U184		
Ethane, 1,1,1,2-tetrachloro-	630206	*	U208		
Ethane, 1,1,2,2-tetrachloro-	79345	*	U209	*	*
Ethanethioamide	62555	*	U218		
Ethane, 1,1,1-trichloro-	71556	*	U226	*	*
Ethane, 1,1,2-trichloro-	79005	*	U227	*	*
Ethanimidothioic acid, 2-(dimethyl-amino-N-hydroxy-2-oxo-, methyl ester (A2213)	30558431	*	U394		
Ethanimidothioic acid, 2-(dimethyl-amino)-N-[[(methylamino) carbonyl]oxy]-2-oxo-, methyl ester (Oxamyl)	23135220	*	P194		
Ethanimidothioic acid, N-[[methyl-amino)carbonyl]oxy]-, methyl ester	16752775	*	P066		

Table I 191

CERCLA Hazardous Substances[n]	CAS #	RCRA Waste[1]	RCRA Waste #	CLEAN WATER ACT[2]	CLEAN AIR ACT[3]
Ethanimidothioic acid, N,N'-[thiobis[(methylimino)carbonyloxy]] bis-, dimethyl ester (Thiodicarb)	59669260	*	U410		
Ethanol, 2-ethoxy-	110805	*	U359		
Ethanol, 2,2'-(nitrosoimino)bis-	1116547	*	U173		
Ethanol, 2,2'-oxybis-, dicarbmate (Diethylene glycol, dicarbamate)	5952261	*	U395		
Ethanone, 1-phenyl-	98862	*	U004		*
Ethene, chloro-	75014	*	U043	*	*
Ethene, 2-chloroethoxy-	110758	*	U042	*	
Ethene, 1,1-dichloro-	75354	*	U078	*	*
Ethene, 1,2-dichloro-(E)	156605	*	U079	*	
Ethene, tetrachloro-	127184	*	U210	*	*
Ethene, Trichloro-	79016	*	U228	*	*
Ethion	563122			*	
Ethyl acetate	141786	*	U112		
Ethyl acrylate	140885	*	U113		*
Ethylbenzene	100414			*	*
Ethyl carbamate	51796	*	U238		*
Ethyl chloride	75003			*	*
Ethyl cyanide	107120	*	P101		
Ethylenebisdithiocarbamic acid, salts and esters	111546	*	U114		
Ethylenediamine	107153			*	
Ethylenediamine-tetraacetic acid (EDTA)	60004			*	
Ethylene dibromide	106934	*	U067	*	*

CERCLA Hazardous Substances[n]	CAS #	RCRA Waste[1]	RCRA Waste #	CLEAN WATER ACT[2]	CLEAN AIR ACT[3]
Ethylene dichloride	107062	*	U077	*	*
Ethylene glycol	107211				*
Ethylene glycol monoethyl ether	110805	*	U359		
Ethyleneimine	151564	*	P054		*
Ethylene oxide	75218	*	U115		*
Ethylenethiourea	96457	*	U116		*
Ethyl ether	60297	*	U117		
Ethylidene dichloride	75343	*	U076	*	*
Ethyl methacrylate	97632	*	U118		
Ethyl methanesulfonate	62500	*	U119		
Famphur	52857	*	P097		
Ferric ammonium citrate	1185575			*	
Ferric ammonium oxalate	2944674			*	
Ferric chloride	7705080			*	
Ferric fluoride	7783508			*	
Ferric nitrate	10421484			*	
Ferric sulfate	10028225			*	
Ferrous ammonium sulfate	10045893			*	
Ferrous chloride	7758943			*	
Ferrous sulfate	7720787			*	
Fine mineral fibers[c]	N.A.				*
Fluoranthene	206440	*	U120	*	
Fluorene	86737			*	
Fluorine	7782414	*	P056		
Fluoracetamide	640197	*	P057		
Fluoracetic acid, sodium salt	62748	*	P058		
Formaldehyde	50000	*	U122	*	*
Formic acid	64186	*	U123	*	

Table I 193

CERCLA Hazardous Substances"	CAS #	RCRA Waste[1]	RCRA Waste #	CLEAN WATER ACT[2]	CLEAN AIR ACT[3]
Fulminic acid, mercury (2+)salt	628864	*	P065		
Fumaric acid	110178			*	
Furan	110009	*	U124		
furan, tetrahydro-	109999	*	U213		
2-Furancarboxaldehyde	98011	*	U125	*	
2,5-Furandione	108316	*	U147	*	*
Furfural	98011	*	U125	*	
Furfuran	110009	*	U124		
Glucopyranose, 2-deoxy-2-(methyl-3-nitrosoureido)-	18883664	*	U206		
D-Glucose, 2-deoxy-2-[[(methyl-nitrosoamino)-car-bonyl]amino]-	18883664	*	U206		
Glycidylaldehyde	765334	*	U126		
Glycol ethers[d]	N.A.				*
Guanidine, N-methyl-N'-nitro-N-nitroso-	70257	*	U163		
Guthion	86500			*	
HALOETHERS	N.A.			*	
HALOMETHANES	N.A.			*	
Heptachlor	76448	*	P059	*	*
HEPTACHLOR AND METABOLITES	N.A.			*	
Heptachlor epoxide	1024573			*	
Hexachlorobenzene	118741	*	U127	*	*
Hexachlorobutadiene	87683	*	U128	*	*
HEXACHLOROCYCLOHEXANE (all isomers)	608731			*	
Hexachlorocyclohexane (gamma isomer)	58899	*	U129	*	*

CERCLA Hazardous Substances[n]	CAS #	RCRA Waste[1]	RCRA Waste #	CLEAN WATER ACT[2]	CLEAN AIR ACT[3]
Hexachlorocyclopentadiene	77474	*	U130	*	*
Hexachloroethane	67721	*	U131	*	*
Hexachlorophene	70304	*	U132		
Hexachloropropene	1888717	*	U243		
Hexaethyl tetraphosphate	757584	*	P062		
Hexamethylene-1,6-diisocyanate	822060				*
Hexamethylphosphoramide	680319				*
Hexane	110543				*
Hexone	108101	*	U161		*
Hydrazine	302012	*	U133		*
Hydrazine, 1,2-diethyl-	1615801	*	U086		
Hydrazine, 1,1-dimethyl-	57147	*	U098		*
Hydrazine, 1,2-dimethyl-	540738	*	U099		
Hydrazine, 1,2-diphenyl-	122667	*	U109	*	*
Hydrazine, methyl-	60344	*	P068		*
Hydrazinecarbothioamide	79196	*	P116		
Hydrochloric acid	7647010			*	*
Hydrocyanic acid	74908	*	P063	*	
Hydrofluoric acid	7664393	*	U134	*	*
Hydrogen chloride	7647010			*	*
Hydrogen cyanide	74908	*	P063	*	
Hydrogen fluoride	7664393	*	U134	*	*
Hydrogen phosphide	7803512	*	P096		*
Hydrogen sulfide	7783064	*	U135	*	
Hydrogen sulfide H2S	7783064	*	U135	*	
Hydroperoxide, 1-methyl-1-phenyl-ethyl-	80159	*	U096		
Hydroquinone	123319				*

Table I 195

CERCLA Hazardous Substances[n]	CAS #	RCRA Waste[1]	RCRA Waste #	CLEAN WATER ACT[2]	CLEAN AIR ACT[3]
2-Imidazolidinethione	96457	*	U116		*
Indeno(1,2,3-cd)pyrene	193395	*	U137	*	
Iron,tris(dimethylcarbamodithioato-S,S')-(Ferbam)	14484641	*	U396		
Iodomethane	74884	*	U138		*
1,3-isobenzofurandione	85449	*	U190		*
Isobutyl alcohol	78831	*	U140		
Isodrin	465736	*	P060		
Isophorone	78591			*	*
Isoprene	78795			*	
Isopropanolamine dodecylbenzene-sulfonate	42504461			*	
Isosafrole	120581	*	U141		
3(2H)-Isoxazolone, 5-(amino-methyl)-	2763964	*	P007		
Kepone	143500	*	U142	*	
Lasiocarpine	303344	*	U143		
Lead	7439921			*	
Lead acetate	301042	*	U144	*	
Lead compounds	N.A.			*	*
Lead arsenate	7784409 7645252 10102484			*	
Lead, bis(acetatato-O)tetra-hydroxytri-	1335326	*	U146		
Lead chloride	7758954			*	
Lead fluoborate	13814965			*	
Lead fluoride	7783462			*	

CERCLA Hazardous Substances[††]	CAS #	RCRA Waste[1]	RCRA Waste #	CLEAN WATER ACT[2]	CLEAN AIR ACT[3]
Lead iodide	10101630			*	
Lead nitrate	10099748			*	
Lead phosphate	7446277	*	U145		
Lead stearate	1072351			*	
Lead subacetate	1335326	*	U146		
Lead sulfate	7446142			*	
Lead sulfide	1314870			*	
Lead thiocyanate	592870			*	
Lindane	58899	*	U129	*	*
Lindane (all isomers)	58899	*	U129	*	*
Lithium chromate	14307358			*	
Malathion	121755			*	
Maleic acid	110167			*	
Maleic anhydride	108316	*	U147	*	*
Maleic hydrazide	123331	*	U148		
Malononitrile	109773	*	U149		
Manganese, bis(dimethylcarbamodi-thioato-S,S')- (Manganese dimethyldithiocarbamate)	15339363	*	P196		
Manganese Compounds	N.A.				*
MDI	101688				*
Melphalan	148823	*	U150		
MEK	78933	*	U159		*
Mercaptodimethur	20332657			*	
Mercuric cyanide	592041			*	
Mercuric nitrate	10045940			*	
Mercuric sulfate	7783359			*	
Mercuric thiocyanate	592858			*	
Mercurous nitrate	10415755			*	

Table I   197

CERCLA Hazardous Substances"	CAS #	RCRA Waste[1]	RCRA Waste #	CLEAN WATER ACT[2]	CLEAN AIR ACT[3]
Mercury	7439976	*	U151	*	*
Mercury Compounds	N.A.			*	*
Mercury, (acetate-O)phenyl-	62384	*	P092		
Mercury fulminate	628864	*	P065		
Methacrylonitrile	126987	*	U152		
Methanamine, N-methyl-	124403	*	U092	*	
Methanamine, N-methyl-N-nitroso	62759	*	P082	*	*
Methane, bromo-	74839	*	U029	*	*
Methane, chloro-	74873	*	U045	*	*
Methane, chloromethoxy-	107302	*	U046		*
Methane, dibromo	74953	*	U068		
Methane, dichloro-	75092	*	U080	*	*
Methane, dichlorodifluoro-	75718	*	U075		
Methane, iodo-	74884	*	U138		*
Methane, isocyanato-	624839	*	P064		*
Methane, oxybis(chloro-	542881	*	P016		*
Methanesulfenyl chloride, trichloro-	594423	*	P118		
Methanesulfonic acid, ethyl ester	62500	*	U119		
Methane, tetrachloro-	56235	*	U211	*	*
Methane, tetranitro-	509148	*	P112		
Methane, tribromo-	75252	*	U225	*	*
Methane, trichloro-	67663	*	U044	*	*
Methane, trichlorofluoro-	75694	*	U121		
Methanethiol	74931	*	U153	*	
Methanimidamide, N,N-dimethyl-N' -[3-[[(methylamino)carbonyl]oxyl- phenyl]-,monohydrochloride (Formetanate hydrochloride)	23422539	*	P198		

CERCLA Hazardous Substances[tt]	CAS #	RCRA Waste[1]	RCRA Waste #	CLEAN WATER ACT[2]	CLEAN AIR ACT[3]
Methanimidamide, N,N-dmethyl-N'-[2-methyl-4-[[(methylamino)carbonyl]oxy]phenyl]-(Formparanate)	17702577	*	P197		
6,9-Methano-2,4,3-benzodi-oxathiepin, 6,7,8,9,10,10-hexa-chloro-1,5,5a,6,9,9a, hexahydro-, 3-oxide	115297	*	P050	*	
1,3,4-Metheno-2H-cyclobutal[cd]pentalen-2-one, 1,1a,3,3a,4, 5,5,5a, 5b,6-decachloroctahydro-	143500	*	U142	*	
4,7-Methano-1H-indene, 1,4,5,6,7, 8,8-heptachloro-3a,4,7,7a-tetra-hydro-	76448	*	P059	*	*
4,7-Methano-1H-indene, 1,2,4,5,6, 7,8,8-octachloro-2,3,3a,4,7,7a-hexahydro-	57749	*	U036	*	*
Methanol	67561	*	U154		*
Methapyrilene	91805	*	U155		
Methomyl	16752775	*	P066		
Methoxychlor	72435	*	U247	*	*
Methyl alcohol	67561	*	U154		*
2-Methyl aziridine	75558	*	P067		*
Methyl bromide	74839	*	U029	*	*
1-Methylbutadiene	504609	*	U186		
Methyl chloride	74873	*	U045	*	*

Table I 199

CERCLA Hazardous Substances[tt]	CAS #	RCRA Waste[1]	RCRA Waste #	CLEAN WATER ACT[2]	CLEAN AIR ACT[3]
Methyl chlorocarbonate	79221	*	U156		
Methyl chloroform	71556	*	U226	*	*
Methyl chloroformate	79221	*	U156		
3-Methylcholanthrene	56495	*	U157		
4,4'-Methylenebis(2-chloroaniline)	101144	*	U158		*
Methylene bromide	74953	*	U068		
Methylene chloride	75092	*	U080	*	*
4,4'-Methylenedianiline	101779				*
Methylene diphenyl diisocyanate	101688				*
Methyl ethyl ketone	78933	*	U159		*
Methyl ethyl ketone peroxide	1338234	*	U160		
Methyl hydrazine	60344	*	P068		*
Methyl iodide	74884	*	U138		*
Methyl isobutyl ketone	108101	*	U161		*
Methyl isocyanate	624839	*	P064		*
2-Methyllactonitrile	75865	*	P069	*	
Methylmercaptan	74931	*	U153	*	
Methyl methacrylate	80626	*	U162	*	*
Methyl parathion	298000	*	P071	*	
4-Methyl-2-pentanone	108101	*	U161		*
Methyl tert-butyl ether	1634044				*
Methylthiouracil	56042	*	U164		
Mevinphos	7786347			*	
Mexacarbate	315184			*	
Mitomycin C	50077	*	U010		
MNNG	70257	*	U163		
Monoethylamine	75047			*	
Monomethylamine	74895			*	

CERCLA Hazardous Substances"	CAS #	RCRA Waste[1]	RCRA Waste #	CLEAN WATER ACT[2]	CLEAN AIR ACT[3]
Multi Source Leachate	NONE	*	F039		
Muscimol	2763964	*	P007		
Naled	300765			*	
5,12-Naphthacenedione, 8-acetyl-10-[3-amino-2,3,6-trideoxy-alpha-L-lyxo-hexopyranosyl)oxy]-7,8,9,10-tetrahydro-6,8,11-trihydroxy-1-methoxy-, (8S-cis)-	20830813	*	U059		
1-Naphthalenamine	134327	*	U167		
2-Naphthalenamine	91598	*	U168		
Naphthalenamine, N,N'-bis (2-chloroethyl)-	494031	*	U026		
Naphthalene	91203	*	U165	*	*
Naphthalene, 2-chloro-	91587	*	U047	*	
1,4-Naphthalenedione	130154	*	U166		
2,7-Naphthalenedisulfonic acid, 3, 3'-[(3,3'-dimethyl-(1,1'-biphenyl)-4,4'-diyl)-bis(azo)]bis(5-amino-4-hydroxy)-tetrasodium salt	72571	*	U236		
Naphthenic acid	1338245			*	
1,4-Naphthoquinone	130154	*	U166		
alpha-Naphthylamine	134327	*	U167		
beta-Naphthylamine	91598	*	U168		
alpha- Naphthylthiourea	86884	*	P072		
Nickel	7440020			*	
Nickel ammonium sulfate	15699180			*	
Nickel Compounds	N.A.			*	*
Nickel carbonyl	13463393	*	P073		

Table I 201

CERCLA Hazardous Substances[n]	CAS #	RCRA Waste[1]	RCRA Waste #	CLEAN WATER ACT[2]	CLEAN AIR ACT[3]
Nickel carbonyl Ni(CO)4, (T-4)-	13463393	*	P073		
Nickel chloride	7718549			*	
Nickel cyanide	557197	*	P074		
Nickel cyanide Ni(CN)2	557197	*	P074		
Nickel hydroxide	12054487			*	
Nickel nitrate	14216752			*	
Nickel sulfate	7786814			*	
Nicotine, & salts	54115	*	P075		
Nitric acid	7697372			*	
Nitric acid, thallium (1+)salt	10102451	*	U217		
Nitric oxide	10102439	*	P076		
p-Nitroaniline	100016	*	P077		
Nitrobenzene	98953	*	U169	*	*
4-Nitrobiphenyl	92933				*
Nitrogen dioxide	10102440	*	P078	*	
Nitrogen oxide NO	10102439	*	P076		
Nitrogen oxide NO2	10102440	*	P078	*	
Nitroglycerine	55630	*	P081		
Nitrophenol (mixed)	25154556			*	
m-Nitrophenol	554847			*	
o-Nitrophenol	88755			*	
p-Nitrophenol	100027	*	U170	*	*
2-Nitrophenol	88755			*	
4-Nitrophenol	100027	*	U170	*	*
NITROPHENOLS	N.A.			*	
2-Nitropropane	79469	*	U171		*
NITROSAMINES	N.A.			*	
N-Nitrosodi-n-butylamine	924163	*	U172		

CERCLA Hazardous Substances[tt]	CAS #	RCRA Waste[1]	RCRA Waste #	CLEAN WATER ACT[2]	CLEAN AIR ACT[3]
N-Nitrosodiethanolamine	1116547	*	U173		
N-Nitrosodiethlamine	55185	*	U174		
N-Nitrosodimethylamine	62759	*	P082	*	*
N-Nitrosodiphenylamine	86306			*	
N-Nitroso-N-ethylurea	759739	*	U176		
N-Nitroso-N-methylurea	684935	*	U177		*
N-Nitroso-N-methylurethane	615532	*	U178		
N-Nitrosomethylvinylamine	4549400	*	P084		
N-Nitrosomorpholine	59892				*
N-Nitrosopiperidine	100754	*	U179		
N-Nitrosopyrrolidine	930552	*	U180		
Nitrotoluene	1321126			*	
m-Nitrotoluene	99081				
o-Nitrotoluene	88722				
p-Nitrotoluene	99990				
5-Nitro-o-toluidine	99558	*	U181		
Octamethylpyrophosphoramide	152169	*	P085		
Osmium oxide OsO4 (T-4)-	20816120	*	P087		
Osmium tetroxide	20816120	*	P087		
7-Oxabicyclo[2.2.1]heptane-2,3-dicarboxylic acid	145733	*	P088		
1,2-Oxathiolane, 2,2-dioxide	1120714	*	U193		*
2H-1,3,2-Oxazaphosphorin-2-amine, N,N-bis(2-chloroethyl) tetra-hydro-, 2-oxide	50180	*	U058		
Oxirane	75218	*	U115		*
Oxiranecarboxyaldehyde	765344	*	U126		
Oxirane, (chloromethyl)-	106898	*	U041	*	*

Table I 203

CERCLA Hazardous Substances[tt]	CAS #	RCRA Waste[1]	RCRA Waste #	CLEAN WATER ACT[2]	CLEAN AIR ACT[3]
Paraformaldehyde	30525894			*	
Paraldehyde	123637	*	U182		
Parathion	56382	*	P089	*	*
PCBs	1336363			*	*
Aroclor 1016	12674112			*	*
Aroclor 1221	11104282			*	*
Aroclor 1232	11141165			*	*
Aroclor 1242	53469219			*	*
Aroclor 1248	12672296			*	*
Aroclor 1254	11097691			*	*
Aroclor 1260	11096825			*	*
PCNB	82688	*	U185		*
Pentachlorobenzene	608935	*	U183		
Pentachloroethane	76017	*	U184		
Pentachloronitrobenzene	82688	*	U185		*
Pentalchlorophenol	87865	*	U242	*	*
1,3-Pentadiene	504609	*	U186		
Perchloroethylene	127184	*	U210	*	*
Phenacetin	62442	*	U187		
Phenanthrene	85018			*	
Phenol	108952	*	U188	*	*
Phenol, 2-chloro-	95578	*	U048	*	
Phenol, 4-chloro-3-methyl-	59507	*	U039	*	
Phenol, 2-cyclohexyl-4,6-dinitro-	131895	*	P034		
Phenol, 2,4-dichloro-	120832	*	U081	*	
Phenol, 2,6-dichloro-	87650	*	U082		
Phenol, 4,4'-(1,2-diethyl-1,2-ethenediyl)bis-,(E)	56531	*	U089		

CERCLA Hazardous Substances"	CAS #	RCRA Waste[1]	RCRA Waste #	CLEAN WATER ACT[2]	CLEAN AIR ACT[3]
Phenol, 2,4-dimethyl	105679	*	U101	*	
Phenol, 2,4-dinitro	51285	*	P048	*	*
Phenol, methyl-	1319773	*	U052	*	*
Phenol, 2-methyl-4,6-dinitro-,& salts	534521	*	P047	*	*
Phenol, 2,2'-methylenebis[3,4,6-trichloro-	70304	*	U132		
Phenol, 3-(1-methylethyl)-,methyl carbamate (m-Cu-menyl methyl-carbamate)	64006	*	P202		
Phenol, 2-(1 methylpropyl)-4,6-dinitro	88857	*	P020		
Phenol, 3-methyl-5-(1-methylethyl)-methyl carbamate (Promecarb)	2631370	*	P201		
Phenol, 4-nitro-	100027	*	U170	*	*
Phenol, pentachloro	87865	*	U242	*	*
Phenol, 2,3,4,6-tetrachloro-	58902	*	U212		
Phenol, 2,4,5-trichloro-	95954	*	U230	*	*
Phenol, 2,4,6-trichloro-	88062	*	U231	*	*
Phenol, 2,4,6-trinitro-,ammonium salt	131748	*	P009		
L-Phenylalanine, 4-[bis(2-chloro-ethyl)aminol]	148823	*	U150		
p-Phenylenediamine	106503				*
1,10-(1,2-Phenylene)pyrene	193395	*	U137	*	
Phenylmercury acetate	62384	*	P092		
Phenylthiourea	103855	*	P093		
Phorate	298022	*	P094		
Phosgene	75445	*	P095	*	*

Table I   . 205

CERCLA Hazardous Substances[n]	CAS #	RCRA Waste[1]	RCRA Waste #	CLEAN WATER ACT[2]	CLEAN AIR ACT[3]
Phosphine	7803512	*	P096		*
Phosphoric acid	7664382			*	
Phosphoric acid, diethyl 4-nitro-phenyl ester	311455	*	P041		
Phosphoric acid, lead(2+) salt (2:3)	7446277	*	U145		
Phosphorodithioic acid, O,O-diethyl S-[2-(ethylthio)ethyl]ester	298044	*	P039	*	
Phosphorodithioic acid, O,O-diethyl S-(ethylthio), methyl ester	298022	*	P094		
Phosphorodithioic acid, O,O-diethyl S-methyl ester	3288582	*	U087		
Phosphorodithioic acid, O,O-dimethyl S-[2(methylamino)-2-oxoethyl] ester	60515	*	P044		
Phosphorofluoridic acid, bis(1-methylethyl) ester	55914	*	P043		
Phosphorothioic acid, O,O-diethyl O-(4-nitrophenyl) ester	56382	*	P089	*	*
Phosphorothioic acid, O,[4-[(di-methylamino) sulfonyl]phenyl] O, O-dimethyl ester	52857	*	P097		
Phosphorothioic acid, O,O-dimethyl O-(4-nitrophenyl) ester	298000	*	P071	*	
Phosphorothioic acid, O,O-diethyl O-pyrazinyl ester	297972	*	P040		
Phosphorus	7723140			*	*
Phosphorus oxycloride	10025873			*	
Phosphorus pentasulfide	1314803	*	U189	*	
Phosphorus sulfide	1314803	*	U189	*	

CERCLA Hazardous Substances[n]	CAS #	RCRA Waste[1]	RCRA Waste #	CLEAN WATER ACT[2]	CLEAN AIR ACT[3]
Phosphorus trichloride	7719122			*	
PHTHALATE ESTERS	N.A.			*	
Phthalic anhydride	85449	*	U190		*
2-Picoline	109068	*	U191		
Piperidine, 1-nitroso-	100754	*	U179		
Piperidine, 1,1'-(tetrethiodicarbono-thioyl)-bis-(Bis(pentamenthylene) thiuram tetrasulfide)	120547	*	U400		
Plumbane, tetraethyl-	78002	*	P110	*	
POLYCHLORINATED BIPHENYLS	1336363			*	*
Aroclor 1016	12674112			*	*
Aroclor 1221	11104282			*	*
Aroclor 1232	11141165			*	*
Aroclor 1242	53469219			*	*
Aroclor 1248	12672296			*	*
Aroclor 1254	11097691			*	*
Aroclor 1260	11096825			*	*
Polycyclic Organic Matter	N.A.				*
POLYNUCLEAR AROMATIC HYDROCARBONS	N.A.			*	
Potassium arsenate	7784410			*	
Potassium arsenite	10124502			*	
Potassium bichromate	7778509			*	
Potassium chromate	7789006			*	
Potassium cyanide	151508	*	P098	*	
Potassium cyanide K(CN)	151508	*	P098	*	
Potassium hydroxide	1310583			*	
Potassium permanganate	7722647			*	

Table I 207

CERCLA Hazardous Substances"	CAS #	RCRA Waste[1]	RCRA Waste #	CLEAN WATER ACT[2]	CLEAN AIR ACT[3]
Potassium silver cyanide	506616	*	P099		
Pronamide	23950585	*	U192		
Propanal, 2-methyl-2-(methylthio)-O-[(methylamino)carbonyl]oxime	116063	*	P070		
1-Propanamine	107108	*	U194		
1-Propanamine, N-propyl-	142847	*	U110		
1-Propanamine,N-nitroso-N-propyl-	621647	*	U111	*	
Propane,2-nitro	79469	*	U171		*
1,3-Propane sultone	1120714	*	U193		*
Propane, 1,2-dibromo-3-chloro	96128	*	U066		*
Propane, 1,2-dichloro-	78875	*	U083	*	*
Propanedinitrile	109773	*	U149		
Propanenitrile	107120	*	P101		
Propanenitrile, 3-chloro-	542767	*	P027		
Propanenitrile, 2-hydroxy-2-methyl-	75865	*	P069	*	
Propane, 2,2'-oxybis[2-chloro-	108601	*	U027	*	
1,2,3-Propanetriol, trinitrate-	55630	*	P081		
1-Propanol, 2,3-dibromo-, phosphate (3:1)	126727	*	U235		
1-Propanol, 2-methyl-	78831	*	U140		
Propanol, 2-methyl-2-(methyl-sulfonyl)-,O-[(methylamino)carbonyl]oxime (Aldicarb sulfone)	1646884	*	P203		
2-Propanone	67641	*	U002		
2-Propanone, 1-bromo-	598312	*	P017		
Propargite	2312358			*	
Propargyl alcohol	107197	*	P102		
2-Propenal	107028	*	P003	*	*
2-Propenamide	79061	*	U007		*

CERCLA Hazardous Substances[n]	CAS #	RCRA Waste[1]	RCRA Waste #	CLEAN WATER ACT[2]	CLEAN AIR ACT[3]
1-Propene, 1,1,2,3,3,3-hexachloro-	1888717	*	U243		
1-Propene, 1,3-dichloro-	542756	*	U084	*	*
2-Propenenitrile	107131	*	U009	*	*
2-Propenenitrile, 2-methyl-	126987	*	U152		
2-Propenoic acid	79107	*	U008		*
2-Propenoic acid, ethyl ester	140885	*	U113		*
2-Propenoic acid, 2-methyl-,ethyl ester	97632	*	U118		
2-Propenoic acid, 2-methyl-, methyl ester	80626	*	U162	*	*
2-Propen-1-ol	107186	*	P005	*	
beta-Propiolactone	57578				*
Propionaldehyde	123386				*
Propionic acid	79094			*	
Propionic acid, 2-(2,4,5-trichloro-phenoxy)-	93721	*	U233	*	
Propionic anhydride	123626			*	
Propoxur (Baygon)	114261				*
n-Propylamine	107108	*	U194		
Propylene dichloride	78875	*	U083	*	*
Propylene oxide	75569			*	*
1,2-Propylenimine	75558	*	P067		*
2-Propyn-1-ol	107197	*	P102		
Pyrene	129000			*	
Pyrethrins	121299 121211 8003347			*	
3,6-Pyridazinedione, 1,2-dihydro	123331	*	U148		
4-Pyridinamine	504245	*	P008		

Table I 209

CERCLA Hazardous Substances[n]	CAS #	RCRA Waste[1]	RCRA Waste #	CLEAN WATER ACT[2]	CLEAN AIR ACT[3]
Pyridine	110861	*	U196		
Pyridine, 2-methyl-	109068	*	U191		
Pyridine, 3-(1-methyl-2-pyrrolidinyl)-,(S)-	54115	*	P075		
2,4-(1H,3H)-Pyrimidinedione, 5-[bis (2-chloroethyl)amino]-	66751	*	U237		
4(1H)-Pyrimidinone, 2,3-dihydro-6-methyl-2-thioxo-	56042	*	U164		
Pyrrolidine, 1-nitroso	930552	*	U180		
Pyrrolo[2,3-b] indol-5-ol, 1,2,3,3a, 8,8a-hexahydro-1,3a8-trimethyl-, methylcarbamate (ester), (3aS-cis)- (Physostigmine)	57476	*	P204		
Quinoline	91225			*	*
Quinone	106514	*	U197		*
Quintobenzene	82688	*	U185		*
Radionuclides (including radon)	N.A.				*
Reserpine	50555	*	U200		
Resorcinol	108463	*	U201	*	
Saccharin and salts	81072	*	U202		
Safrole	94597	*	U203		
Selenious acid	7783008	*	U024		
Selonious acid, dithallium (1+) salt	12039520	*	P114		
Selenium	7782492			*	
Selenium Compounds	N.A.			*	*
Selenium dioxide	7446084	*	U204	*	
Selenium oxide	7446084	*	U204	*	
Selenium Sulfide	7488564	*	U205		
Selenium sulfide SeS2	7488564	*	U205		

CERCLA Hazardous Substances"	CAS #	RCRA Waste[1]	RCRA Waste #	CLEAN WATER ACT[2]	CLEAN AIR ACT[3]
Selenourea	630104	*	P103		
L-Serine, diazoacetate (ester)	115026	*	U015		
Silver	7440224			*	
SILVER AND COMPOUNDS	N.A.			*	
Silver cyanide	506649	*	P104		
Silver cyanide Ag (CN)	506649	*	P104		
Silver nitrate	7761888			*	
Silvex (2,4,5-TP)	93721	*	U233	*	
Sodium	7440235	.		*	
Sodium arsenate	7631892			*	
Sodium arsenite	7784465			*	
Sodium azide	26628228	*	P105		
Sodium bichromate	10588019			*	
Sodium bifluoride	1333831			*	
Sodium bisulfite	7631905			*	
Sodium chromate	7775113			*	
Sodium cyanide	143339	*	P106	*	
Sodium cyanide Na (CN)	143339	*	P106	*	
Sodium dodecylbenzenesulfonate	25155300			*	
Sodium fluoride	7681494			*	
Sodium hydrosulfide	16721805			*	
Sodium hydroxide	1310732			*	
sodium hypochlorite	7681529 10022705			*	
Sodium methylate	124414			*	
Sodium nitrite	7632000			*	
Sodium phosphate, dibasic	7558794 10039324 10140655			*	

Table I 211

CERCLA Hazardous Substances[tt]	CAS #	RCRA Waste[1]	RCRA Waste #	CLEAN WATER ACT[2]	CLEAN AIR ACT[3]
Sodium phosphate, tribasic	7601549			*	
	7758294				
	7785844				
	10101890				
	10124568				
	10361894				
Sodium selenite	10102188			*	
	7782823				
Streptozotocin	18883664	*	U206		
Strontium chromate	7789062			*	
Strychnidin-10-one	57249	*	P108	*	
Strychnidin-10-one,2,3,-dimethoxy-	357573	*	P018		
Strychnine, & salts	57249	*	P108	*	
Styrene	100425			*	*
Styrene oxide	96093				*
Sulfur monochloride	12771083			*	
Sulfur phosphide	1314803	*	U189	*	
Sulfuric acid	7664939			*	
Sulfuric acid, dithallium (1+) salt	7446186	*	P115	*	
Sulfuric acid, dimethyl ester	77781	*	U103		*
2,4,5-T acid	93765	*	U232	*	
2,4,5-T amines	2008460			*	
	1319728				
	3813147				
	6369966				
	6369977				

CERCLA Hazardous Substances"	CAS #	RCRA Waste[1]	RCRA Waste #	CLEAN WATER ACT[2]	CLEAN AIR ACT[3]
2,4,5-T esters	93798			*	
	1928478				
	2545597				
	25168154				
	61792072				
2,4,5-T salts	13560991			*	
2,4,5-T	93765	*	U232	*	
TCDD	1746016			*	*
TDE	72548	*	U060	*	
1,2,4,5-Tetrachlorobenzene	95943	*	U207		
2,3,7,8-Tetrachlorodibenzo-p-dioxin	1746016			*	*
1,1,1,2-Tetrachloroethane	630206	*	U208		
1,1,2,2-Tetrachloroethane	79345	*	U209	*	*
Tetrachloroethene	127184	*	U210	*	*
Tetrachloroethylene	127184	*	U210	*	*
2,3,4,6-Tetrachlorophenol	58902	*	U212		
Tetraethyl lead	78002	*	P110	*	
Tetraethyl pyrophosphate	107493	*	P111	*	
Tetraethyldithiopyrophosphate	3689245	*	P109		
Tetrahydrofuran	109999	*	U213		
Tetranitromethane	509148	*	P112		
Tetraphosphoric acid, hexaehtyl ester	757584	*	P062		
Thallic oxide	1314325	*	P113		
Thallium	7440280			*	
Thallium and compounds	N.A.			*	

Table I 213

CERCLA Hazardous Substances"	CAS #	RCRA Waste[1]	RCRA Waste #	CLEAN WATER ACT[2]	CLEAN AIR ACT[3]
Thallium (l) acetate	563688	*	U214		
Thallium (l) carbonate	6533739	*	U215		
Thallium (l) chloride	7791120	*	U216		
Thallium chloride TICI	7791120	*	U216		
Thallium (l) nitrate	10102451	*	U217		
Thallium oxide TI203	1314325	*	P113		
Thallium selenite	12039520	*	P114		
Thallium (l) sulfate	7446186 10031591	*	P115	*	
2H-1,3,5-Thiadiazine-2-thione, tetrahydro-3,5-dimethyl-(Dazomet)	533744	*	U366		
Thioacetamide	62555	*	U218		
Thiodiphosphoric acid, tetraethyl ester	3689245	*	P109		
Thiofanox	39196184	*	P045		
Thioimidodicarbonic diamide [(H2N)C(S)] 2NH	541537	*	P049		
Thiomethanol	74931	*	U153	*	
Thioperxoydicarbonic diamide [(H2N)C(S)] 2S2, tetramethyl-	137268	*	U244		
Thioperoxydicarbonic diamide, tetrabutyl (Tetrabutylthiuram di-sulfide)	1634022	*	U402		
Thioperoxydicarbonic diamide, tetraethyl (Disulfiram)	97778	*	U403		
Thiophenol	108985	*	P014		
Thiosemicarbazide	79196	*	P116		
Thiourea	62566	*	U219		

CERCLA Hazardous Substances"	CAS #	RCRA Waste[1]	RCRA Waste #	CLEAN WATER ACT[2]	CLEAN AIR ACT[3]
Thiourea, (2-chlorophenyl)-	5344821	*	P026		
Thiourea, 1-naphthalenyl-	86884	*	P072		
Thiourea, phenyl-	103855	*	P093		
Thiram	137268	*	U244		
Titanium tetrachloride	7550450				*
Toluene	108883	*	U220	*	*
Toluenediamine	95807 496720 823405 25376458	*	U221		*
2,4-Toluene diamine	95807 496720 823405 25376458	*	U221		*
Toluene diisocyanate	91087 584849 26471625	*	U223		*
2,4, -Toluene diisocyanate	91087 584849 26471625	*	U223		*
o-Toluidine	95534	*	U328		*
p-Toluidine	106490	*	U353		
o-Toluidine hydrochloride	636215	*	U222		
Toxaphene	8001352	*	P123	*	*
2,4,5-TP acid	93721	*	U233	*	
2,4,5-TP esters	32534955			*	
1H-1,2,4-Triazol-3-amine	61825	*	U011		
Trichlorfon	52686			*	

Table I 215

CERCLA Hazardous Substances"	CAS #	RCRA Waste[1]	RCRA Waste #	CLEAN WATER ACT[2]	CLEAN AIR ACT[3]
1,2,4-Trichlorobenzene	120821			*	*
1,1,1-Trichloroethane	71556	*	U226	*	*
1,1,2-Trichloroethane	79005	*	U227	*	*
Trichloroethene	79016	*	U228	*	*
Trichloroethylene	79016	*	U228	*	*
Trichloromethanesulfenyl chloride	594423	*	P118		
Trichloromonofluoromethane	75694	*	U121		
Trichlorophenol	25167822			*	
2,3,4-Trichlorophenol	15950660				
2,3,5-Trichlorophenol	933788				
2,3,6-Trichlorophenol	933755				
2,4,5-Trichlorophenol	95954	*	U230	*	*
2,4,6-Trichlorophenol	88062	*	U231	*	*
3,4,5-Trichlorophenol	609198				
Triethanolamine dodecylbenzene-sulfonate	27323417			*	
Triethylamine	121448			*	*
Trifluralin	1582098				*
Trimethylamine	75503			*	
2,2,4-Trimethylpentane	540841				*
1,3,5-Trinitrobenzene	99354	*	U234		
1,3,5-Trioxane, 2,4,6-trimethyl-	123637	*	U182		
Tris(2,3-dibromopropyl) phosphate	126727	*	U235		
Trypan blue	72571	*	U236		
Unlisted Hazardous Wastes Characteristic of Corrosivity	N.A.	*	D002		
Unlisted Hazardous Wastes Characteristic of Toxicity		*			

CERCLA Hazardous Substances"	CAS #	RCRA Waste[1]	RCRA Waste #	CLEAN WATER ACT[2]	CLEAN AIR ACT[3]
Arsenic	N.A.	*	D004		
Barium	N.A.	*	D005		
Benzene	N.A.	*	D018	*	*
Cadmium	N.A.	*	D006		
Carbon Tetrachloride	N.A.	*	D019	*	
Chlordane	N.A.	*	D020	*	
Chlorobenzene	N.A.	*	D021	*	
Chloroform	N.A.	*	D022	*	
Chromium	N.A.	*	D007		
o-Cresol	N.A.	*	D023		
m-Cresol	N.A.	*	D024		
p-Cresol	N.A.	*	D025		
Cresol	N.A.	*	D026		
2,4-D	N.A.	*	D016	*	
1,4-Dichlorobenzene	N.A.	*	D027	*	
1,2-Dichloroethane	N.A.	*	D028	*	
1,1-Dichloroethylene	N.A.	*	D029	*	
2,4-Dinitrotoluene	N.A.	*	D030	*	
Endrin	N.A.	*	D012	*	
Heptachlor (and epoxide)	N.A.	*	D031	*	
Hexachlorobenzene	N.A.	*	D032	*	
Hexachlorobutadiene	N.A.	*	D033	*	
Hexachloroethane	N.A.	*	D034	*	
Lead	N.A.	*	D008		
Lindane	N.A.	*	D013	*	
Mercury	N.A.	*	D009		
Methoxychlor	N.A.	*	D014	*	
Methyl ethyl ketone	N.A.	*	D035		
Nitrobenzene	N.A.	*	D036	*	

Table I 217

CERCLA Hazardous Substances"	CAS #	RCRA Waste[1]	RCRA Waste #	CLEAN WATER ACT[2]	CLEAN AIR ACT[3]
Pentachlorophenol	N.A.	*	D037	*	
Pyridine	N.A.	*	D038		
Selenium	N.A.	*	D010		
Silver	N.A.	*	D011		
Tetrachloroethylene	N.A.	*	D039	*	
Toxaphene	N.A.	*	D015	*	
Trichloroethylene	N.A.	*	D040	*	
2,4,5-Trichlorophenol	N.A.	*	D041	*	
2,4,6-Trichlorophenol	N.A.	*	D042	*	
2,4,5-TP	N.A.	*	D017	*	
Vinyl chloride	N.A.	*	D043	*	*
Unlisted Hazardous Wastes Characteristic of Ignitability	N.A.	*	D001		
Unlisted Hazardous Wastes Characteristic of Reactivity	N.A.	*	D003		
Uracil mustard	66751	*	U237		
Uranyl acetate	541093			*	
Uranyl nitrate	10102064		.	*	
Urea, N-ethyl-N-nitroso-	759739	*	U176		
Urea, N-methyl-N-nitroso	684935	*	U177		*
Urethane	51796	*	U238		*
Vanadic acid, ammonium salt	7803556	*	P119		
Vanadium oxide V205	1314621	*	P120	*	
Vanadium pentoxide	1314621	*	P120	*	
Vanadyl sulfate	27774136			*	
Vinyl acetate	108054			*	*
Vinyl acetate monomer	108054			*	*
Vinylamine, N-methyl-N-nitroso	4549400	*	P084		
Vinyl bromide	593602				*

Environmental Crime

CERCLA Hazardous Substances[n]	CAS #	RCRA Waste[1]	RCRA Waste #	CLEAN WATER ACT[2]	CLEAN AIR ACT[3]
Vinyl chloride	75014	*	U043	*	*
Vinylidene chloride	75354	*	U078	*	*
Warfarin, & salts, when present at concentrations greater than 0.3%	81812	*	P001		
Xylene	1330207	*	U239	*	*
m-Xylene	108383				*
o-Xylene	95476				*
p-Xylene	106423				*
Xylene (mixed)	1330207	*	U239	*	*
Xylenes (isomers and mixture)	1330207	*	U239	*	*
Xylenol	1300716			*	
Yohimban-16-carboxylic acid, 11,17-dimethoxy-18-[(3,4,5-trimethoxy-benzoyl)oxy]-, methyl ester (3beta, 16beta,17alpha,18beta, 20alpha)-	50555	*	U200		
Zinc	7440666			*	
ZINC AND COMPOUNDS	N.A.			*	
Zinc acetate	557346			*	
Zinc ammonium chloride	52628258			*	
Zinc, bis(dimethylcarbomodithioato-S,S')-, (Ziram)	137304	*	P205		
Zinc, bis(diethylcarbamodithioato-S,S')-(Ethyl Ziram)	14324551	*	U407		
Zinc borate	1332076			*	
Zinc bromide	7699458			*	
Zinc carbonate	3486359			*	
Zinc chloride	7646857			*	
Zinc cyanide	557211	*	P121	*	

Table I 219

CERCLA Hazardous Substances"	CAS #	RCRA Waste[1]	RCRA Waste #	CLEAN WATER ACT[2]	CLEAN AIR ACT[3]
Zinc cyanide Zn(CN)2	557211	*	P121	*	
Zinc fluoride	7783495			*	
Zinc formate	557415			*	
Zinc hydrosulfite	7779864			*	
Zinc nitrate	7779886			*	
Zinc phenosulfonate	127822			*	
Zinc phosphide	1314847	*	P122	*	
Zinc phosphide Zn3P2, when present at concentrations greater than 10%.	1314847	*	P122	*	
Zinc Silicofluoride	16871719			*	
Zinc sulfate	7733020			*	
Zirconium nitrate	13746899			*	
Zirconium potassium fluoride	16923958			*	
Zirconium sulfate	14644612			*	
Zirconium tetrachloride	10026116			*	

1. Resource Conservation and Recover Act, Section 3001.

2. Clean Water Act, Sections 311(b)(4), 307(a).

3. Clean Air Act, Section 112.

†Table source is 40 CFR 302.4.

††Also included as hazardous substances are those hazardous wastes from Non-Specific Sources ('F' Wastes, 40 CFR 261.31) and from Specific Sources ('K' Wastes, 40 CFR 261.32).

Table II
55-Gallon Drum Conversion Chart
Inches to Gallons

Inches	Gallons	Inches	Gallons
1.0	1.72	17.5	30.12
1.5	2.58	18.0	30.98
2.0	3.44	18.5	31.84
2.5	4.30	19.0	32.70
3.0	5.16	19.5	33.56
3.5	6.02	20.0	34.42
4.0	6.88	20.5	35.28
4.5	7.75	21.0	36.14
5.0	8.61	21.5	37.01
5.5	9.47	22.0	37.87
6.0	10.33	22.5	38.73
6.5	11.19	23.0	39.59
7.0	12.05	23.5	40.45
7.5	12.91	24.0	41.31
8.0	13.77	24.5	42.17
8.5	14.63	25.0	43.03
9.0	15.49	25.5	43.89
9.5	16.35	26.0	44.75
10.0	17.21	26.5	45.61
10.5	18.07	27.0	46.47
11.0	18.93	27.5	47.33
11.5	19.79	28.0	48.19

Table II 221

Inches	Gallons	Inches	Gallons
12.0	20.65	28.5	49.05
12.5	21.51	29.0	49.91
13.0	22.38	29.5	50.78
13.5	23.24	30.0	51.64
14.0	24.10	30.5	52.50
14.5	24.96	31.0	53.36
15.0	25.82	31.5	54.22
15.5	26.68	32.0	55.08
16.0	27.54	32.5	55.94
16.5	28.40	33.0	56.80
17.0	29.26	33.5	57.66

INDEX

A

Aerial photography, 8, 41 (*see also*
  Surveillance methodology)
Air sampling, 9–10
Analytical methods, 122, 129, 130–31, 133,
  134
  corrosivity, 133
  ignitability, 134
  toxicity, 129, 130–31
Appendix
  alpha table of hazardous substances and
    statutory authority, 167–232
  bibliography and footnotes, 165–66
  conversion chart for 55-gallon drums,
    233–34
  glossary of environmental crime investiga-
    tions terminology, 157–64
  Standard Operating Procedures for
    Environmental Crime Unit, 149–56

B

Building inspection records
  hazardous vapor venting systems, 14
Building inspections
  chemical stains on parking lots, 7
  discharge pipe installation diggings, 8
  drum rings, 49
  employee interviews, 61
  excavations, recent, 8
  exterior storm drains, 52–53
  exterior wall plating line stains, 7
  ground stains, 53
  leaching pools, 7, 52–53, 141
  liquid streams from waste storage areas, 7
  roof, 53
  sunken or depressed areas, 8, 53
  trash receptacles, 19, 53
  waste discharge points, 47–51, 56
Building plans and usage, 18, 20, 41, 75 (*see
  also* Probable cause development)
Business records, 17–20

C

Certificates of Incorporation, 17
Chain-of-custody, 28, 70–71, 93, 101, 118,
  125
Chemical analysis, 11, 62, 77, 91–92, 121–35,
  121–35 (*see also* Sampling methods)
  analytical methods, 122, 129, 131, 133, 134
    (*see also* Analytical methods)
  laboratory certification, 121–23
    chain-of-custody protocols, 125
    method certification, 124
    personnel credentials, 125
    postanalysis activities, 126
    sample holding time requirements, 125
    testing methodology, 121–22
  instrumentation and methodology, 126–35
    gas chromatograph/mass spectrometer,
      127–29
    inductively coupled plasma/atomic emis-
      sions spectrometer, 129–31
    inductively coupled plasma/optical emis-
      sions spectrometer, 129
    Pensky-Martens closed-cup tester, 133–34
    pH meter, 132–33
Chemical evidence-gathering, 11, 62, 77,
  91–92, 93–120 (*see also* Sampling methods)
  chain-of-custody, 28, 70–71, 93, 101, 118,
    125
  labeling, 116
  log book, 117–18
  photographing, 116
  sealing, 117
Chemical products (raw) inventory, 34, 62,
  87, 111
Chemical suppliers records, 18–19, 62, 87
  (*see also* Probable cause development)
Chemist, forensic, 36
Citizen suits, vii
Computerized databases
  Criminal Pointer System, 17
  Emergency Planning and Community

223

Right-To-Know Act, 15
Hazardous Waste Manifest System, 15–16
Regional Associations Information
    Network, 16–17
worker's compensation, 17
Confined space regulations, 13
Contamination
    chemical sampling, 106–7, 117–19
Covert surveillance, 13, 41 (*see also*
    Surveillance methodology)
Crime scene coordinator, 24–25, 35, 36,
    68–69
Criminal environmental investigations, xi,
    3–6, 7–63, 65–82, 137–47
    (*see also* Environmental crime scene;
        Hazardous waste abandonment)
    criminal violations, vii, xi
    equipment list, 4, 22–23, 38, 72, 97
    hazardous waste abandonment, 65–82
    hazmat response team, 5–6, 26, 69
    investigative files, 147
    search-warrant investigations, 7–63
    site investigation team, 36–44, 67–71
    standard operating procedures, 5, 35–44,
        149–56
    sting operations, 137–47
    training, 3
Criminal Pointer System, 17

D
Decontamination team, 5, 26, 39, 69–70
Department of Transportation
    drum labeling requirements, 89–91
Discharge Monitoring Reports, 11
Drums
    drum rings, 49
    drum-tracing, 60–61, 83–92
    drum volume, 112
Drum-tracing investigations, 83–92
    chemical analysis, 91–92
    container, 87–91 (*see also* Labels)
        Dept. of Transportation information,
            89–91
        labels, 87
            chemical buyers directory, 87
            manufacturer, 87
            motive, 89
            writing on drum, 88
    person or persons, 86

fingerprints, 86
footprints, 86
physical evidence, other, 86
    hand tools, 86
    invoices, 86
    register receipts, 86
vehicle identification, 83–85
    tire tracks, 84
    vehicle contamination, 85
    vehicle size, 84
    witnesses, 83
Dye testing, 34, 56

E

Electron ionization, 99–100, 128
Elemental analysis, 129–31
Emergency Planning and Community Right-
    To-Know Act database, 15
Entrapment, 137
Environmental crime scene
    communications, 43, 77
    equipment list, 4, 22–23, 38, 72, 97
    gathering of physical evidence, 3, 6, 28, 37,
        73–82, 93–120
    sampling methods, 93–120
    hazardous materials personnel
        backup team, 5, 26, 69
        decontamination team and facilities, 5,
            26, 39, 69–70
        medical team, 27, 39, 70
        safety officer, 5, 25–26, 35, 36, 69–70
        sampling team, 28, 46–47, 70 (*see also*
            Sampling methods)
    hazardous waste abandonment, 65–82,
        83–92
    investigative files, 147
    motive and knowledge, 28, 89, 140
    search-warrant team, 23–34 (*see also* Search-
        warrant team)
    site investigation, interior and exterior,
        47–53, 73–82
    site investigation team, 36–37, 67–71
    standard operating procedures, 5, 149–56
    surreptitious entry, 59–60
    surveillance, 7 (*see also* Surveillance
        methodology)
Environmental crime suspect
    interview, 63

Environmental discharges
  air sampling, 9–10
  hazardous waste discharges, 11–13 (*see also*
    Hazardous waste abandonment)
  dye test team, 34, 56
  environmental crime scene investiga-
    tions, 47–53, 65–82
  identification of contaminants, 7, 71 (*see also*
    Sampling methods)
Environmental enforcement associations,
  regional, 16
Environmental prosecutions, viii
Environmental Protection Agency training
  programs
  criminal environmental investigations, 3
  hazardous materials incident response, 3
  hazardous materials sampling, 3 (*see also*
    Sampling methods)
Environmental search warrant (*see* Search
  warrants)
Equipment list, 4, 22–23, 38, 72, 97
  analytical methodology, 122, 129, 130–31,
    133, 134
Evidence methodology
  abandoned hazardous wastes, 65–82
  chemical analysis, 121–35
  environmental crime scene investigations,
    47–53
  sampling operation, 40, 46–47, 70–71,
    93–120
  sampling resources, 6, 28, 37
  search warrant planning methodology,
    21–23, 28
Expected protection levels, 38

F
Field blank bottle, 106
Field tests and equipment, 98–101
  acids or caustics, pH test, 98
  complex chemical mixtures, Dräeger-Tube
    detection system, 101
  flammable substances, LEL meter, 99
  metal presence, x-ray fluorescent detector,
    100
  organic compounds, flame ionization
    detector, 99
  organic compounds, photo-ionization
    detector, 100
  oxygen displacement, oxygen meter, 99

  radioactive materials, Geiger counter
Fire inspection records
  hazardous chemicals inventory, 14

H
Hazardous materials
  crime scene criteria, 5, 65
    backup team, 5, 69
    decontamination team and facilities, 5,
      26, 39, 69–70
    safety officer, 5, 25–26, 35, 36, 69–70
  Emergency Planning and Community
    Right-To-Know Act database, 15
  environmental crime scene investigation,
    47–53, 65–82
  post-search interviews, 61, 63
  identification by air sampling, 9–10
  regulatory files, 14–15
  waste discharges, 11–13
    dye test, 34, 56
Hazardous Materials Response Team, 5–6,
  26, 69 (*see also* Search-warrant team)
  Emergency Planning and Community
    Right-To-Know Act database, 15
  fire or police jurisdiction, 6
Hazardous vapor discharges, 14
Hazardous waste abandonment, 65–82
  abandoned trailer investigations, 78–79
    off-loading techniques, 78–79
    trailer exterior examination, 78
  contaminated waste water procedures, 74
  crime scene treatment and security, 67–79
  equipment list, 72
  evidence gathering tasks in hot zone, 73–76
    chemical evidence, 77–78
  hazardous waste tanker investigations,
    79–82
    driver interview, 80
    field tests, 81
    manifests and permits, 80
    placards, 80
    tanker discharges, 81
  physical evidence and documentation,
    67–69, 70–71, 73–76, 93–120
    coliwasa tube examination, 76, 108
    contaminated waste water, 74
    hazardous waste containers, 74–76
  postsearch briefing, 77, 94
  site investigation team, 68–71 (*see also*

Search-warrant team)
  chain of command, 67–68
  crime-scene coordinator, 68–69
  laboratory team and science officer, 71
  safety team and officer, 69–70
    decontamination team, 69–70
    hazmat backup team, 69
    medical team, 70
  sample team, 70
  notification procedures, 67
  waste abandonment examples, 65, 66
Hazardous waste discharges, 11–13 (*see also*
  Hazardous waste abandonment)
  covert entry into sewer system, 13
  dye test, 34, 56
  environmental crime scene investigation,
    47–53
  hazardous waste container markings, 60–61
  portable liquid samplers, 11–12
  trace evidence, 11
Hazardous waste management, 14, 15–16, 74
Hazardous Waste Manifest System, 14, 15–16
Hazardous waste sting operations, 137–47
  entrapment issues, 137
  illegal hazardous waste generators, 137,
    141–47
    audio and video surveillance, 143, 144
    criminal transaction, 144
    establishing as transporter, 141, 144
    hazardous wastes manifest and disposal,
      146–47
    limitations on types of waste disposal, 142
    office requirements and equipment
      inventory, 142, 144
    personnel requirements, 142–43
      chemical evidence team, 143
      hazardous waste transportation team,
        43
      surveillance team, 143
    post-transport waste examination, 145
    standard operating procedure re haz-
      ardous
      waste disposal, 142
    use of informant, 141, 143
    vehicle, 143–44
  illegal hazardous waste transporters,
    137–41
    establishing undercover generator, 139
      audio and video surveillance, 139–40

  office requirements, 139–40
  hazardous waste containers, 140
    contents, waste substance options,
      138–39
    drum markings, 140
    labeling, international poison symbol,
      140
    labeling, written warnings, 140
  hazardous waste removal, 140–41
    search warrant, 141
    surveillance photography, 140
  sting operation planning, 138–39, 141–42
    investigative files, 147
    legal ramifications of using nonhaz-
      ardous waste, 138

I
Ignitability, 96, 133–34
Industries
  auto body shops, 10, 37
  circuit board manufacturing, 10, 37
  dry cleaning operations, 10, 37
  furniture refinishers, 10, 37
  plating operations, 10, 37
  printing operations, 10, 37
Interview team, 33–34 (*see also* Search-warrant team)
  information requests, 33

L
Labels
  chemical suppliers records, 18–19, 62, 87
Laboratory analysis of chemical evidence,
  62, 77
Laboratory team and science officer, 27–28,
  35, 36, 71
Laws, burden of proof, 28, 89, 105–6
Laws, compliance, 13, 19, 40
Liquid samplers, 11–12
Logbook, 117–18

M
Material Safety Data Sheets, 29–30, 37, 62,
  111
Motive and knowledge, 28, 89

N
National Pollutant Discharge Elimination
  System, ix

O

OSHA, 15

P

Physical evidence
air sampling, 9–10
chain-of-custody, 28, 70–71, 93, 101, 118
chemical sampling, 77, 93–120
covert sampling, 13
dye test, 34, 56
environmental crime scene investigation,
47–53, 65–82
equipment list, 4, 22–23, 38, 72, 97
hazardous waste discharges, 11–13
hazardous waste container markings,
60–61, 74
sampling operation, 40, 46–47, 76
sampling team, 28, 37, 69–70
Probable cause development, 7–21
building plans, 18, 41
chemical suppliers records, 18
hazardous waste management files, 15–16
property records, 18
regulatory files, 14–15 (*see also* Regulatory
files)
surveillance, 7–13 (*see also* Surveillance
methodology)
remote, 8
typical, 7–8
worker's compensation records, 17
Property records, 17 (*see also* Regulatory files;
Records team)
evidence of knowledge and/or intent, 28
documents to be seized, 29–33
accident records, 32
environmental surveys, 31
equipment logs, 32
hazardous waste manifests, 30–31
Material Safety Data Sheets, 29, 62
personnel records, 32
raw chemical product purchases, 30
regulatory reports and correspondence,
31
removal procedures under search warrant,
28–29
Publicly Owned Treatment Works, 11, 13,
31–32

R

Records team, 17 (*see also* Search-warrant
team)
documents to be seized, 29–33 (*see also*
Property records)
accident records, 32
environmental surveys, 31
equipment logs, 32
hazardous waste manifests, 30–31
Material Safety Data Sheets, 29, 62
personnel records, 32
raw chemical product purchases, 30
regulatory reports and correspondence,
31
evidence of knowledge and/or intent, 28,
31
application of self-audit privilege guide
lines, 31–32
removal procedures under search warrant,
28–29
search procedures and documentation,
28–29
Regulatory files
air permits, 14
building inspection records, 14
fire inspection records, 14
fire department records, 14
hazardous waste management files, 14
health department inspection records, 14
local water board records, 14
state environmental agency files 14
waste water discharge permits, 14
Representative sample, 108 (*see also*
Sampling methods and analysis)
Resources
safety resources, 5, 26–27, 67
hazmat team, 5–6, 26, 69
sampling resources, 6, 28, 37, 70

S

Safety team, 25–27, 35 36, 69–70 (*see also*
Search-warrant team)
decontamination team, 26, 39, 69–70
hazmat backup team, 26, 69
medical team, 27, 39, 70
Sampling methods and analysis, 21, 28, 36,
40, 46–47, 55–57, 71, 77–78, 93–120

air sampling, 9–10
chemical evidence-gathering, 11, 55–57, 77, 91–92, 93–120
  analysis request sheet, 118
  chain-of-custody, 28, 70–71, 93, 101, 118
  chemical sampling, 104–8
  labeling, 116
  log book, 117–18
  photographing, 116
  sealing, 117
  shipping to lab for analysis, 119–20
  transporting from crime scene, 119
chemical sampling, 104–8
  analytical test selection, 105–6
  field blank bottle, 106
  glove changes, 107
  legal requirements for proof, 105
  representative samples, 108
  trace chemical analysis, 105, 109–11 (*see also* sampling analysis)
  trip blank bottle, 106
contamination, 106–7
covert sampling, 13
dye testing, 34, 56
field tests and equipment, 98–101
  acids or caustics, pH test, 98
  complex chemical mixtures, Dräeger-Tube detection system, 101
  flammable substances, LEL meter, 99
  metal presence, x-ray fluorescent detector, 100
  organic compounds, flame ionization detector, 99
  organic compounds, photo-ionization detector, 100
  oxygen displacement, oxygen meter, 99
  radioactive materials, Geiger counter
liquid samplers, 11–13
sampling analysis, 97–98
  list of analytical parameters, 98
  trace analysis, 105, 109–11
    elbows and traps, 110
    pipes, pumps, hoses, 109
    raw product, 111
    vent pipes, chimneys, stacks, 110
sampling documentation, list, 101–4
sampling equipment, 93
  sample container identification and preparation, 94–96

    cyanide, 96
    ignitability determination, 96
    inorganic compounds, 95
    oil and grease, 96
    phenols and polychlorinated biphenyl, 96
    semivolatile organic compounds, 95
    total petroleum hydrocarbons, 96
    volatile organic compounds, 95
  sample device identification and preparation, 96–97
sampling operation, 11, 40, 46–47, 55, 70–71, 93–120
  chain-of-custody, 56, 70–71, 101, 118
  criminal statute requirements, 97, 105
  sample point identification, 55, 77, 103, 104
  sampling order, 55
  split samples, 40
  trace analysis, 105, 109–11
  volume readings, 56, 112
sampling plan determinants, 93–94
  hazardous waste abandonment, 94
  search warrant, 94
sampling team, 6, 28, 36, 46–47, 70
Search warrants, 7–63
  briefing, 35–44
  postsearch briefing, 54, 94
  equipment requirements, 4, 22–23, 38
  intelligence gathering, 22
  personnel requirements, 23–34
  planning, 21–23
    determination of goals, 21
    sampling and analysis, 21, 40, 55
      sample point identification, 55
      sampling order, 55
  postsearch investigation, 61–63
  probable cause development, 7–21
    business records, 17–20
    regulatory files, 14–16 (*see also* Regulatory files)
    surveillance, 7–20 (*see also* Surveillance methodology)
  search-warrant team, 23–34 (*see also* Search-warrant team)
  surreptitious entry, 13, 59–61
  warrant execution, 45–58
  warrant execution briefing, 35–44
    site investigation team, 36–37

warrant execution staging, 44–45
Search-warrant execution, 45–58
  sampling methodology, 21, 28, 36, 40,
    46–47, 55–56
      (*see also* Sampling methods and
      analysis)
  service of warrant protocol, 45
  site security and parking, 46
  site visit by prosecutor, 58
  team deployment and interior search,
    46–51
    exterior search, 52–53
    receipt, 58
Search-warrant team
  chain of command, 23–24, 35
  crime-scene coordinator, 24–25, 35, 36
  interview team, 33–34
  laboratory team and science officer, 27–28,
    35, 36
  records team, 28–29 (*see also* Records
    team)
  safety team and officer, 5, 25–26, 35, 36
    decontamination team, 26, 39
    hazmat backup team, 26
    medical team, 27, 39
  sample team, 28, 36, 37
  site investigation team, 36–44
  site security team, uniformed, 25, 42
Semivolatile organic compounds, 95, 127–29
Site investigation team, 36–37, 68–71
  (*see also* Hazardous materials abandon-
    ment; Search-warrant team)
Standard operating procedures, 5, 35–44,
    142, 149–56
  briefing, 35–44
  full document, 149–56
  procedural topics, 5
Surreptitious entry, 59–60
  disabling security systems, 59–60
  marking hazardous waste containers, 60–61
  surreptitious-entry search warrant, 59–61
Surveillance methodology
  business records, 17–20
  regulatory files, 14–15
  remote, 8–13
    air and sewer samplers, 8, 9–13
      sampling techniques, 10–13
    aerial photography
      air pollution sources, 8

excavation sites, 8
ground stains, 8
illegal activities in progress, 8
manufacturing areas, 8
waste discharge point sources, 8
waste storage, 8
  infrared photography, 8
    heat differentiation, 8
  video photography, 8, 9
sting operations, 137–47
typical, 7–8
  personal witness
    chemical stains on parking lots, 7
    discharge pipe installation diggings, 8
    employee interviews, 61
    excavations, recent, 8
    exterior wall platingline stains, 7
    leaching pools, 7, 141
    liquid streams from waste storage
      areas, 7
    sunken or depressed areas, 8
    vehicle license plate numbers, 8
      employee background investigations,
      8
  still photographs, 7
  videotape, 7
Superfund Amendments
  Title III, 5–6

T
Tankers, hazardous waste investigations,
    79–82
  (*see also* Hazardous waste abandonment)
  driver interview, 80
  field tests, 81
  manifests and permits, 80
  placards, 80
  tanker discharges, 81
Toxicity, 129, 130–131
Trip blank bottle, 106

U
Unemployment records, 17

V
Vapor discharges, 14
Volatile organic compounds, 95, 127–29
Volume readings, 56, 112
  above-ground tanks, 114

below-ground tanks, 115
drums and cans, 112
leaching pools, 113
hazardous waste tankers, 115

W

Waste containers
　marking during surreptitious entry, 60–61
Waste, hazardous (*see* Hazardous waste)

Waste water discharges, 14, 47
　dye test, 34, 56
　environmental crime scene
　exterior investigation, 52–53, 65–82
　interior investigation, 47–51
Weather conditions, 41–42
Worker's compensation, 17 (*see also*
　Computerized databases)
　injured workers' interviews, 61

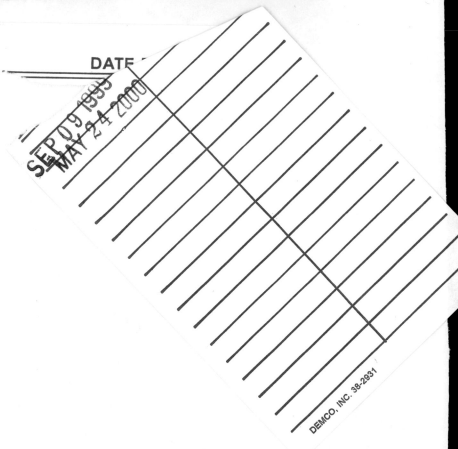